"Bill Grace once had a powerful vision of a world at peace, of people sharing this rock we call Planet Earth. Equally important, he has a long-term track record. For years, he has helped create workplaces, institutions, and communities founded on values essential for global well-being. In this important and wonderfully well-written book, he shares his practical wisdom about how to achieve a just, peaceful, and sustainable world. May it be read and embraced by leaders of many sorts, from parents to teachers to CEOs. It is a book that could make a difference."

—Parker J. Palmer
Author of *A Hidden Wholeness, Let Your Life Speak,*
The Courage to Teach, and *Healing the Heart of Democracy*

"*Sharing the Rock* is timely, profound, inspirational, and hard to put down. It's clearly a lifetime of thinking crafted into a resource for the caring person to sort through the challenges that stand between us, peaceful coexistence with the rest of humanity, and a sustainable future."

—Rick Steves
Host, writer, and producer of popular PBS and
NPR travel shows

"That the world needs leaders and followers who care deeply for the common good is one of those important truisms that are too often ignored. Perhaps this book will bring us back to common sense. Far too long have we wandered in the wilderness of individualism, both theoretically and practically. Grace aims not only to persuade a few readers but to initiate a movement. Should he succeed, his will prove to be the most important book thus far in this century."

—John B. Cobb Jr.
Professor Emeritus, Claremont School of Theology

"What a read! This book is filled with 'think about and do now exercises' so the reader can get an immediate gut check on how he or she measures up as a leader the world needs today. Plus every question posed by the author is supported by a vignette with profound consequences for today's thoughtful reader. Taken seriously, this book can shape new ways of considering and resolving 'old' problems. *Sharing the Rock* is a much welcomed addition to my bookshelf, with great insights into the true nature of leading."

—Jim Maloney, MA, CAE
Cofounder and first board chairman of the National Association
for Community Leadership Organizations

"Bill Grace has sustained a remarkable dedication to the work of ethical leadership on behalf of the common good. In *Sharing the Rock*, he has distilled the insight he has gained and refined. All who have valued his gifts will be inspired again by this book, while others may now meet him for the first time in this 'gracious space' where he invites the reader onto a pathway of meaningful action and hope."

—Sharon Daloz Parks
Leadership for the New Commons
Senior Fellow, Whidbey Institute

"This is the book educators have been waiting for to clarify the vision and to identify the words and examples to help us and our students achieve the moral imperative of education—stewarding and promoting the common good for our global and diverse family. The leadership practices presented in this book offer a practical guide to all who desire to effect change for the common good and who understand the urgency of now."

—Gwendolyn Jordan Dungy
Executive director, NASPA—Student Affairs Administrators
in Higher Education

"*Sharing the Rock* is both a framework for creating a just planet and a poignant reminder, particularly to those in leadership positions, of the values that must be consistently held if we are to break through the all-too-pervasive culture of 'me and mine first.' Bill Grace challenges us all to lead not only with our heads but with hope and conviction that there is in fact a way to achieve a common good."

—Neil Nicoll
President and CEO of the YMCA of the USA

"*Sharing the Rock* is comprehensive and well argued. It is, in fact, a potent template for morally enlightened leadership that serves the common good. Bill Grace guides us to step into our power at a time when each one of us is called upon to create a morally coherent planetary civilization."

—James O'Dea
Visionary activist, international social healer, and
former president of The Institute of Noetic Sciences

"In a time when our nation seems more self-focused than ever, Bill Grace presents a compelling case for a new type of leadership that benefits all."

—Steve Coen
President and CEO of the Kansas Health Foundation

sharing *the* rock

sharing *the* rock

Shaping Our Future through Leadership for the Common Good

Bill Grace

commongood works

Bellevue, Washington

Published by: Common Good Works
14216 SE Eastgate Drive
Bellevue, WA 98006
www.commongoodworks.com

Editor: Carolyn Bond
Copyeditor: Ellen Kleiner
Book design: Ann Lowe
Illustrations: Ann Lowe

Printed and bound in the United States of America

Front cover image © Dpw-shane/Dreamstime.com
Title page image © Indian summer/Dreamstime.com
Hands around the world image © Alexmax/Dreamstime.com

Excerpt from Hans Magnus Enzensberger's poem "song for those who know," in *Selected Poems* © 1999 Sheep Meadow Press, reprinted with permission of Hans Magnus Enzensberger and Sheep Meadow Press.
Mary Oliver's poem "The Journey," in *Dream Work* © 1986 by Mary Oliver, reprinted in its entirety with permission from Grove/Atlantic, Inc.

Library of Congress Cataloging-in-Publication Data

Grace, William J., 1951-

Sharing the rock : shaping our future through leadership for the common good / Bill Grace. — Bellevue, Wash. : Common Good Works, c2011.

p. ; cm.

ISBN: 978-0-9845786-0-3
Includes bibliographical references.

    1. Leadership—Moral and ethical aspects. 2. Common good.
    3. Values. 4. Social change. 5. Social ethics. 6. Business ethics.
    I. Title. II. Title: Shaping our future through leadership for the common good.

HM1261 .G73 2011   2010928457
303.3/4--dc22   1102

1 3 5 7 9 10 8 6 4 2

To Sandy,
our children Nic, Ben, and Wooga—
and all the other children of the world

The Rock

WHILE VISITING JERUSALEM in April 1975, I came close to a prolonged, bitter struggle over a rock. Seeking a place to stay my first evening in the city, I saw a modest building with a sign out front written mostly in Hebrew, which I could not read but containing the English word *hostel,* so I inquired about lodging. The staff welcomed me warmly and showed me to a room.

I got to know the staff as I shared my experiences of exploring Jerusalem with them every evening. Perhaps that is why on the third day of my stay they asked if I would join them for the weekly Shabbat ritual, to which I replied, "I would be honored, especially since I'm not Jewish."

The staff exclaimed, "You're not Jewish? This is a residence for rabbinical students!"

Embarrassed, I apologized and explained how I had misinterpreted the sign.

Laughing, they said that no harm had been done but that I should make plans to move to a nearby youth hostel the next afternoon. I replied that I would visit the Dome of the Rock that morning and return midday to move my things. Their eyes widened with interest. Because the Dome of the Rock, a Muslim site, was off limits for them, they asked if I would describe it when I returned.

Outside in the Old City, my eyes fixed on the striking architecture of the Dome of the Rock, its golden cupola contrasting sharply with the earth-toned structures surrounding it. It is the third holiest shrine in the Muslim world, built over the rock from which Muhammad took his night journey, ascending to heaven on a Buraq—a white, winged horse—accompanied by the Archangel Gabriel. It also rests on the site of Solomon's Temple (known as the first temple) and the second temple of Jerusalem, built after the first was destroyed and the only remaining remnant of which is in the form of the Western Wall, one of Judaism's most sacred places.

Standing at the Western Wailing Wall, the site of the holiest synagogue in the Jewish world, I felt awe as I watched devout Jews offering prayers. Moments later, I climbed the steps to the Temple Mount, the broad platform supporting the Dome of the Rock, entered it, and was equally awed by the beauty of its intricate mosaic work and the reverent faces of Muslims at worship.

Over lunch at the hostel, I described my visit to the Dome of the Rock in detail. As I finished, one of the rabbinical students said, to my surprise, "Did you know that the rock is also the altar where Abraham prepared to sacrifice his son Isaac?" The Jews, he explained, believe that before the Messiah can appear, Solomon's Temple must be rebuilt on that very spot. He left the obvious unsaid: for the temple to be rebuilt, the Dome of the Rock had to be torn down. I thought, "This is the kernel of the conflict in the Middle East—two religions making equal claim to the same sacred rock, unable to share space and thus causing the people of both faiths to suffer."

Late that afternoon, I sat on the tree-shaded hilltop known as the Garden of Gethsemane, where Jesus prayed before the Crucifixion, pondering how this ancient city didn't seem to have enough room for more than one story of faith. All three Abrahamic religions—Judaism, Islam, and Christianity—claim Jerusalem as a holy site, and although they have since divided it into separate quarters these groups, like many siblings, can't get along. I paced around the garden, deeply troubled by the implications of this endless hostility. How will there ever be peace in the Middle East?

Twenty-one years later, in the summer of 1996, I had a profound vision based on this experience that also helped to guide the writing of this book. At the time, my wife, Sandy, our two sons, and I were visiting Sandy's family in Hanska, Minnesota, a peaceful rural town of five hundred people. One morning when Sandy was out with friends and her parents had taken the boys downtown for breakfast, I decided to spend time meditating in the upstairs guestroom. As I sat there quietly, memories associated with the room flooded my awareness. I recalled that on our wedding day in 1979, about an hour before the ceremony, the other men in the wedding party and I had been in this room changing into our tuxedos. That day I had been surrounded by friends and family representing all the stages of my life. Embraced by the warm memories, I experienced a profound joy, which I understood as a gift from Spirit. From the depths of my heart, I said, "Thank you."

Suddenly I heard the voice of Spirit say, in a casual yet enthusiastic tone, "You're welcome." Then I heard an invitation: "Do you want to see something?"

As if this were an ordinary conversation, I replied, "Sure."

Then something remarkable happened. As if by some cinematic special effect, the bedroom in Hanska was stretched upward beyond the earth's atmosphere, from where I saw the entire earth suspended before me in space. Next I heard the question "What do you see?" and answered intuitively, "All one family." The loving spiritual presence surrounding me confirmed the accuracy of my response. Finding myself just as quickly returned to the bedroom in Hanska, I was filled with profound gratitude and said "thank you" again. At that moment, the voice asked if I remembered the question I had pondered back in the Garden of Gethsemane: How will there ever be peace in the Middle East? Then the voice said: "Share the rock." In a flash I found myself back in space, looking again with deep love at the earth, and a second time I heard the words: "Share the rock." Only this time the meaning of the word *rock* expanded to refer to the entire planet some call the third rock from the sun.

Though the whole experience lasted only seconds, it felt timeless and left me amazed, humbled, and forever changed. The more I observed the human and environmental costs of competition for exclusive rights to territory, oil, markets, and power, the more my heart yearned for the day when all humanity would taste the love, peace, and justice I witnessed in that divine encounter in Hanska. Accomplishing such a vision, I soon realized, requires a new kind of leadership—one cast for the specific purpose of ensuring that we share the rock known as earth, our common home, by recognizing that we are all one family—a discovery that inspired the writing of this book.

Contents

Introduction

SHARING THE ROCK is the product of my longtime interest in social justice, a thread in my life that can be traced through a series of influential experiences ranging from early family circumstances to world travel to a thirty-year vocation working to advance social change and leadership for the common good.

I grew up in a unique single-parent, economically poor but educationally stimulating household. My father was a fork-truck driver who had nevertheless received a Jesuit education, majoring in classics, and had knowledge of Latin and Greek. Behind his longshoreman's vocabulary lay the mind of a blue-collar scholar, and he taught me how to look beneath the surface of things and engage in responsible social critique.

During my junior high school and high school years, I, like many teenagers, was socially ostracized. I learned firsthand what it feels like to be a victim of injustice and unkindness, an experience that later made me able to empathize with the pain of others and react with indignation to perceived injustices. When I went to Berkshire Community College in the fall of 1969, however, I found a mentor in John Lambert, professor of environmental studies. His belief in me opened a new door to learning, and his love for the natural world stimulated my interest in the environment, inspiring me to serve as the campus liaison for the first Earth Day, in April 1970. Studying ecology while engaged in environmental activism helped me see that we are all connected in a single web of life and that it is important to encourage new behaviors that respect that reality.

In 1972, as a spectator at the Olympic Games in Munich, I saw the people of the world come together in celebration and unity, only to have this vision shattered by an act of horrific violence—the massacre of Israelis—motivated by religious intolerance. Afterward, I met an elderly Jewish man who encouraged me to visit Dachau, where I experienced, with horror, evidence of the Holocaust. These two events left me wondering how humanity was capable of such cruelty and what could be done to help people treat each other with greater care and concern.

After college, in 1975, I joined a friend on a backpacking trip around the world. I had read about chronic malnutrition, hunger, political oppression of the poor, and lack of religious tolerance, but on this trip I witnessed these conditions directly. I also experienced the kindness of strangers on a daily basis. One compassionate encounter stays with me vividly. In Egypt, I developed sunstroke and was close to death. The owner of the Golden Hotel in Cairo treated me like a son, refusing payment for my room, food, medicine, and doctor visits as he and his staff nursed me back to health over the course of a week. To this day, I remain deeply touched and informed by the care and generosity he showed to a stranger and regard him as an example of goodness made manifest.

Through these life experiences, I saw that humans have the capacity to advance both good and evil. History is filled with stunning examples of both. Although our darker nature is always present, I believe—and educational theory concurs—that individuals and groups alike can intentionally develop virtuous habits of the mind and heart and become active agents for goodness in general and social justice in particular.

While beginning a career as an educator, I also recognized that leadership has the potential to be the most effective means of bringing about needed social change because leadership impacts every field of study and every level of human organization. After I had gained an increased awareness of the need for social change, I began to explore ways in which I could focus more on leadership for the common good and envision a model to involve others in this activity. I saw that we live in an era of possibly grave developments. The earth's environmental systems are extremely stretched, and the world's poor, with their growing sense of the unjust social systems that cause their suffering, are increasingly impatient for change. I realized, however, that this is also a time of unprecedented opportunities that call not for panic or despair but for compassion, imagination, and action. Eventually it became clear to me that what is needed is a new model of leadership, one that can guide our choices and behaviors toward a future where all can thrive. Specifically, we need leadership to foster a new worldview, a common good worldview to replace the divisive us-them worldview that has dominated human history since time immemorial at every level, from local to global.

Sharing the Rock presents such a model of leadership for the common good. The book is an offering to those who aspire to living values-based lives for the good of others, who know that humanity needs to make some big changes fast, and who are looking for a framework for doing both.

Part I of the book explains the common good worldview and why shifting to it is so urgently needed. The most effective way to change a worldview is in terms of the moral stance that undergirds it. A common good worldview registers at the third, or highest, level of moral development identified by development theory, where choices are made based on principle and with concern for the good of all affected by them. In this book, the third level of moral development is called the third circle. When individuals make choices from a third-circle orientation, they can be confident that those decisions are furthering the common good.

Part I also introduces leadership for the common good as the necessary tool for accomplishing this change in worldview, describing the four cornerstones of such leadership: justice, care, inclusiveness, and the moral urgency of acting now since time is short. This leadership model is inclusive in regard to who can be a leader for the common good—not just those who are already in formal leadership positions but anyone who chooses to live according to a third-circle orientation.

Part II presents seven practices of leadership for the common good. Some of these practices, particularly choosing personal values and crafting a vision, are familiar from other leadership models. Others are specific to this model: seeking out resources for social change that are available only in the marginalized parts of society; creating a social environment where all points of view, including the unpopular, are welcome; and cultivating the leader's voice, or genuine expression and action, in bringing about change. This leadership model leaves room for hope as an unshakeable companion for the leader who is willing to move directly into the heart of challenging issues. Finally, the core of this model of leadership for the common good is courage, for in the end it is thoughtful, strategic action driven by courage that brings about the greatest change.

Each chapter in Part II opens with a story highlighting a real person who has done this work well. These chapters also include exercises and reflection questions to assist readers in applying the practices in their own lives as leaders.

sharing *the* rock

Part I

FUNDAMENTALS OF LEADERSHIP
FOR THE COMMON GOOD

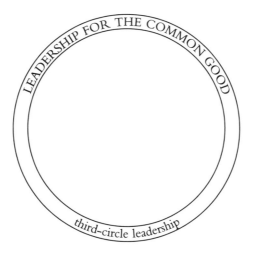

LEADERSHIP FOR THE COMMON GOOD

third-circle leadership

IF WE ARE ALL ONE FAMILY, why not share the earth and its resources so that everyone has enough to live a decent, fulfilling life? This simple idea offers a straightforward if elusive solution to dozens of complex global problems. The common good is a big idea, easily embraced from a perspective miles above the planet, where the wholeness of the earth and interconnectedness of all life cannot be missed. On the ground, it is a harder idea to hold on to.

The common good, however, is ultimately a moral vision, approachable through a moral framework. It aligns with the highest, or third, level of moral development, where choices are governed by principle and inclusiveness. In this book, that third level is referred to as the third circle. The behaviors and choices associated with this moral territory offer a practical way of living that advances the common good.

Bringing the moral behaviors and choices of third-circle orientation to bear on leadership yields four cornerstones of leadership for the common good. Leadership for the common good is the pathway to get us to a future in which everyone on the planet has a sufficient and sustainable lifestyle and humanity is living within a new worldview that mirrors the oneness of the earth.

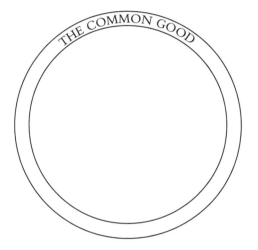

THE COMMON GOOD

1 Shifting to a Common Good Worldview

THE FIRST PHOTOGRAPH of the whole earth from space was taken on December 24, 1968, by the astronauts of *Apollo 8*, the first manned mission to orbit the moon. As the *Apollo 8* capsule emerged from the far side of the moon, crew commander Frank Borman rolled the capsule so its windows and antenna faced the earth to pick up radio reception again with mission control. As he did, our beautiful blue, living planet, set against the dark, cold backdrop of space, appeared above the lunar horizon. Borman exclaimed: "Oh my God! . . . Here's the earth coming up. Wow, is that pretty."[1] He grabbed a black-and-white camera and took a picture, followed by William Anders, who took several color shots. Nature photographer Galen Rowell later described the famous photo "Earthrise," taken by Anders, as "the most influential environmental photograph ever taken."[2]

The view of the earth from space in that photograph irrevocably shifted our collective perspective on who and where we are. It showed us that humanity shares a common home and destiny along with every other form of life on the planet. Viewed from space, clouds flow in broad patterns that touch every portion of the earth, the five great oceans appear as one body of water, and the continents

5

look like puzzle pieces that at one time fit together. Rivers and mountain ranges roam across national boundaries, as do the migratory birds and butterflies that call multiple continents home. Viewed from out in space, the wholeness of our planet is impossible to miss.

Today, more than four decades after the *Apollo 8* voyage, humanity is consciously living in the interconnectedness the first photograph of earth from space revealed to us. Events across the planet are intertwined to a degree unknown in history. Through sophisticated communications and flight technology, we know about happenings in the global community as readily as our grandparents knew what was going on in their hometown. An economic downturn in Asia results in instant price drops on the New York Stock Exchange. Terrorism in England causes the U.S. National Security Agency to raise the threat level to orange. A new flu strain in Mexico affects airplane travel on multiple continents.

Moreover, science has confirmed that we really are all one family. Genetic research now proves that all humans have 100 percent of the same genetic material and, perhaps more humbling, humans share 92 percent of genetic material with all other mammals.

As Martin Luther King Jr. wrote in 1963, "We are tied together in the single garment of destiny, caught in an inescapable network of mutuality."[3] Although he was writing about issues of justice in the United States, today his words apply to global interconnectivity.

Yet even though we are coming to recognize that we are all one global family, humanity's cultural systems and structures, and the beliefs that govern our individual and collective behaviors are not yet in sync with this perspective. They remain based on the assumption of differences between people, an "us" versus "them" perspective.

The us-them framework has operated as the prevailing worldview across cultures throughout human history. Humans have lived in tribes and clans, kingdoms and nations, and have fought over hunting territory, trade routes, religious differences, and access to resources since time immemorial. This perspective has influenced virtually every aspect of human life, including politics, economics, sociocultural institutions, and spirituality.

The us-them worldview has worked well enough for humanity to survive. Today, however, it is our greatest risk. Our weapons have become too powerful and regions of the world too interconnected to be spared the potential dangers resulting from an us-them orientation. The drive on the part of nations having the upper hand to claim and use more than their share of the world's resources has strained the earth's usually resilient ecosystem to the brink of failure. The future depends on whether humanity can shift to a worldview that acknowledges and supports the unity of the global system.

THE COMMON GOOD AS A NEW WORLDVIEW

The essential work of our time is to learn to live together as a global family, caring for one another and sharing the land and resources of our planet. The necessary worldview to achieve this emerges from the ethic of the common good, according to which every member of a community has the inherent right to enjoy the good things of life that the community has to offer, including resources, relationships, and dignity.

As a concept, the common good has a long history. In the fourth century BCE, Aristotle taught that the goal of politics was to create a society that affords a good life for a community of equals. Further, the medieval philosopher Thomas Aquinas believed that leaders care best for the community by enacting laws on behalf of the common good rather than for the good of an elite few. The common good was also a fundamental idea among many Enlightenment writers and philosophers, whose works fueled movements for liberty and equality in Europe and were the basis for the founding documents of the United States. Francis Bellamy, who authored the U.S. Pledge of Allegiance in 1892, capsulized the spirit of the common good in the pledge's final words: "with liberty and justice for all."

As an ethic, the common good has occurred throughout history alongside the dominant ethic of us-them. Just as human communities have fought over differences, they have also looked out for the common good of communities as essential for survival. However, the common good has been practiced mostly *within* groups—such as families, tribes, institutions, and nations—with members sharing resources and supporting one another so the groups remained strong. Thus the common good orientation has historically played a secondary, supporting role to the us-them perspective, which has governed the competitive, and often conflictive, relations *between* groups.

The work before us now is to raise the common good to the level of a worldview by making it the dominant ethic. As a worldview, the common good supports the vision of humanity as all one family. It involves the stewarding of global resources justly and compassionately so that every corner of the earth is a safe place for a child to be born; a place where families, communities, businesses, and the environment can flourish; and a free place where people can govern together. The ideal of global common good is compelling because people sense intuitively that it's right. It's in line with the fundamental wholeness of where we live and who we are.

Making the common good our worldview requires us to invert the existing relationship between us-them and the common good, giving prominence to our commonality and subordinating our differences. Doing this calls for examining the ethical, political, and economic assumptions that shape the nature and quality of public life, including the supremacy of the market economy as we know it. It means embracing a more complex network of social, emotional, and intellectual relationships and a more inclusive view of spirituality. This involves opening ourselves to engage with people we might otherwise avoid and joining with them in moving toward a common future. It also involves learning to manage differing points of view so we enrich the whole without creating divisions. The benefits made possible by a common good worldview—peace, security, and the satisfaction of knowing that we are honoring the inherent wholeness of the created order, in other words, sharing the rock—are well worth the price tag of change.

While making the common good a worldview may seem impossible, this is only because of its comprehensive scope and because it has not yet been dared. Any great human achievement begins with a vision that is inspiring yet daunting and unproved. One of the great visions of the twentieth century was President John F. Kennedy's declaration in 1961 that the United States, by the end of the decade, would put a man on the moon. At the time President Kennedy spoke these words, the technology to accomplish such a task had not yet even been developed. Indeed, one of the remarkable facts about the Apollo program is that NASA learned how to put a man on the moon in the process of doing it.

Shifting worldviews is no less compelling a vision of a preferred future. We do not yet have a detailed and comprehensive description of how and when we will arrive at the common good, but from the vision we can deduce the means that are likely to get us there, and we can let the vision inspire our innovation.

PUTTING THE COMMON GOOD INTO ACTION

Innovative new social programs and projects promoting the common good are already being developed around the world. What they have in common is that they grow out of awareness of the inherent wholeness of the earth and unity of the human family, as well as the realization of our vulnerability on the earth, a tiny island of life with finite resources suspended in a sea of dark space.

Awareness of these ideas is encouraging people to respond with initiatives in many fields, some on a global scale. As Stewart Brand, founder and publisher of the *Whole Earth Catalog*, a publication begun in 1968 that highlights the interconnectedness of earth and humanity, comments: "It is no accident of history that the first Earth Day, in April 1970, came so soon after color photographs of the whole earth from space were made by homesick astronauts on the *Apollo 8* mission to the moon in December 1968. Those riveting Earth photos reframed everything. For the first time humanity saw itself from outside. . . . Suddenly humans had a planet to tend to. The photograph of the whole earth from space helped to generate a lot of behavior—the ecology movement, the sense of global politics, the rise of the global economy, and so on. I think all of those phenomena were, in some sense, given permission to occur by the photograph of the earth from space."[4]

Currently, people the world over are devising initiatives, technologies, and programs involving solutions to social, economic, and environmental problems that make it possible to live on the earth without destroying it or ourselves. Eco-philosopher Joanna Macy calls this comprehensive movement for change directed at the common good the "Great Turning," the heart of which she defines as "a shift from an industrial growth society, dependent on accelerating consumption of resources, to a sustainable or life-sustaining society."[5]

One important initiative conceived on a global scale is the Millennium Development Goals. In September 2000, the largest assembly ever of world leaders gathered for the Millennium Summit at United Nations headquarters in New York City to consider the role of this organization as the world ushered in the new millennium. A key concern articulated in the summit's Millennium Declaration was how to address global inequities: "We recognize that, in addition to our separate responsibilities to our individual societies, we have a collective responsibility to uphold the principles of human dignity, equality and equity at the global level. As leaders we have a duty therefore to all the world's people, especially the most vulnerable and, in particular, the children of the world, to whom the future belongs."[6]

The following eight Millennium Development Goals, set to be achieved by 2015 and supported by all member states of the United Nations plus more than twenty international organizations, read like a list of what it would take to advance the common good in every corner of the world:

1. Eradicate extreme poverty and hunger
2. Achieve universal primary education
3. Promote gender equality and empower women
4. Reduce child mortality
5. Improve maternal health
6. Combat HIV/AIDS, malaria, and other diseases
7. Ensure environmental sustainability
8. Develop a global partnership for development

Another worldwide initiative inspired by the beginning of the millennium is Jubilee 2000, a call for debt forgiveness for impoverished developing nations. The program was based on the biblical concept of the Jubilee year, during which debts were forgiven and social equity restored. As a result of Jubilee 2000, the International Monetary Fund and the World Bank have granted debt relief to twenty-two of the world's most debt-ridden countries.

Other innovations focused on the common good are born of a global awareness but implemented on a local scale. Two prominent examples are the environmental, or green, movement and the organic farming movement, which maintain that every family who recycles plastic bottles or buys produce grown without pesticides contributes to the care of the earth's air, soil, and inhabitants. A related innovation is community-supported agriculture, in which individual consumers or families pledge financial support to a local farm operation in exchange for fresh produce and other foodstuffs supplied through the growing season. Since such farms operate locally, they avoid using the fossil fuels for transportation of food-stuffs and the packaging materials that are part of the standard gro-cery retail system. They also foster a sense of community between consumers and farmers, since no middlemen take a portion of the profits. A further innovation based on the common good is the co-housing movement, in which residents in intentional collaborative communities live in separate homes but share common facilities, with the purpose of conserving resources as well as supporting a rich, interactive community life.

The world of business is also changing. In the United States, the Business Alliance for a Local Living Economy (BALLE), a network of socially responsible local businesses, is dedicated to aligning commerce with the common good. BALLE's vision is to create "within a generation . . . a global system of human-scale, interconnected Local Living Economies that function in harmony with local ecosystems, meet the basic needs of all people, support just and democratic societies, and foster joyful community life."[7]

Internationally, one of the fast-growing business innovations is fair trade, a market-based movement to promote equity in trade as well as sustainability in developing countries. Focused especially on exports such as coffee, tea, handicrafts, chocolate, and produce, fair trade companies offer direct market access to marginalized produc-ers, which means higher wages as well as improved living standards. At the same time, consumers in developed countries can more directly support hardworking people and social initiatives in devel-oping countries. In 2007, fair trade benefited more than 7.5 million producers worldwide.[8]

These innovations, in addition to celebrating community, re-connecting people with the earth, and advancing justice for the least fortunate, are signs of the new common good worldview emerging. The work of our time is to increase the numbers of individuals, institutions, and nations participating in such behaviors and throw open the doors of creativity to increase the panoply of innovations currently underway. In addition to these vital public actions, progress toward a new common good worldview is dependent on personal inner growth that will support even more sweeping progress toward a better future.

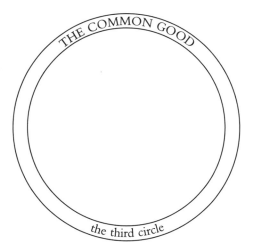

THE COMMON GOOD

the third circle

2 Living from the Third Circle

BECAUSE A WORLDVIEW is comprehensive, involving such aspects as economic, social, and political assumptions and language, it is possible to shift to a common good worldview through any one of these channels—for instance, through a new sociopolitical concept or a new movement for economic change. The most effective way to change a worldview, however, is through the moral stance that undergirds it, because every field of human endeavor is based on moral assumptions.

Every choice we make that determines our actions is grounded, consciously or unconsciously, in a moral stance. When we become conscious of the moral stance that informs our choice-making, we can intentionally advance a new, preferred worldview rather than making default choices that support the old worldview. Shifting to a common good worldview thus requires basing our choices on moral assumptions that support the common good.

MORAL DEVELOPMENT THEORY

According to moral developmental theorists, all individuals are born with the inclination to mature morally as their lives progress.

This happens naturally as long as individuals have a supportive social environment, much the way a corn seed will naturally develop into a cornstalk that produces ears of corn as long as it receives adequate nutrients, water, and sunlight.

Lawrence Kohlberg, working in the 1960s and 1970s, was the first to propose a three-level model of moral development, which he based on the maturing person's changing relationship with social conventions and particularly the person's sense of justice.[1] At the first level, which Kohlberg termed *pre-conventional*, people's choice-making is motivated by personal interests only, what they want or need.

At the second, or *conventional*, level, people's choice-making is driven by the conventions of society, by what other people determine is necessary or just. Their orientation is to existing rules, laws, and beliefs, to what others in their life think is right. People at this level of moral development stop at red lights, return library books on time, and are often responsible citizens. But while such an orientation is necessary for maintenance of the group, it has surprising limitations, for instance, if the group's standards are themselves immoral.

At the third, or *post-conventional,* level, people's choice-making is motivated by principles of what's most just in a given situation. Principles provide a stable moral reference point that gives people a higher-order perspective. Rather than responding to narrow self-interest or being tossed about by the winds of popular culture, people at the third level of moral development are rooted in moral standards that are not influenced by personal interest or social pressure.

In the early 1980s, feminist psychologist Carol Gilligan, a colleague of Kohlberg's, extended his model to make it more gender sensitive.[2] She pointed out that Kohlberg's research celebrated justice as the highest order ethic but dismissed an equally important ethic—care. Her research revealed that moral sensibility develops in terms of both justice and care, with justice being the more masculine aspect and care the more feminine, although men and women readily exercise both in their choice-making.

Developmental theorists like Kohlberg and Gilligan have focused their research primarily on the standards by which people make moral choices. Less attention has been given to the question of who benefits from these choices. Even so, the choice-making associated with each of the three levels of moral development is paired with a corresponding beneficiary.

 Self-oriented choice-making is meant to benefit personal interests only. Choice-making that supports the conventions of a society is usually good for in-groups—for families, institutions, or nations that maintain those norms—but injurious to those on the periphery of that society. Such choice-making tends to benefit a chosen few at the expense of the many. Principle-oriented choice-making, however, is directed to the good of all who are impacted by the choices.

The choice-making characterized by these three orientations can be illustrated by the following scenario. Picture three teenagers in a local corner store individually considering the same choice, whether to steal a candy bar, and all three deciding not to steal one. Although they made the same decision, they had different motivations for their choices. The first teenager thought, "I won't steal it because I don't want to go to jail." This is self-oriented reasoning—I don't want something bad to happen to me. The second teenager thought, "I won't steal it because I don't want to disappoint my parents." This is social-oriented reasoning—deferring to norms established by a group, often parents, teachers, a boss, or peers. The third teenager thought, "Stealing is wrong. If I owned this store, I would not want anybody to steal from me, so I won't steal from the owner." This is principle-oriented reasoning—not stealing because it is unfair and would harm others.

THE THIRD CIRCLE

The three orientations of moral choice-making and their corresponding beneficiaries can be represented effectively as three concentric circles. The increasing area of each circle corresponds to people's increasing moral awareness and maturation, as well as their expanding concern for the diverse members of a community. The third circle marks a qualitative shift from the concerns of the first and second circles and is the only territory from which the shift to a common good worldview can happen.[3]

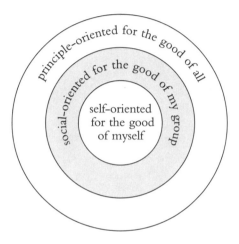

We see the third-circle orientation—the combination of adherence to principle and concern for all—reflected in choices made by the world's great leaders. For example, in spite of China's takeover of Tibet and inhumane treatment of Tibetans the Dalai Lama describes the people of China as his brothers and sisters, maintaining a distinction between the policies of the Chinese government, which he staunchly opposes, and China's citizens. Similarly, the group Rabbis for Human Rights, established in Israel in 1988, seeks to remind the Israeli government of the best parts of the Jewish faith, and in that context they advance the rights and interests of the least fortunate and most vulnerable in Israel—including Palestinians, foreign workers, and women.

Another example of a leader who habitually made choices from the third circle is Abraham Lincoln. Near the end of the Civil War, when General Godfrey Weitzel took charge of the defeated confederate city of Richmond, Virginia, he asked President Lincoln how he should treat the people of Richmond, to which Lincoln replied, referencing a wrestling term as a former grappler himself, "Let 'em up easy."[4]

He thereby showed that he intended to put into action the famous words from his second inaugural address, delivered in 1865, shortly before the war ended: "With malice toward none, with charity for all, with firmness in the right as God gives us to see the right, let us strive on to finish the work we are in, to bind up the nation's wounds, to care for him who shall have borne the battle and for his widow and his orphan, to do all which may achieve and cherish a just and lasting peace among ourselves and with all nations."[5]

It is easy to think of first-, second-, and third-circle choice-making as mutually exclusive, but in fact third-circle concerns encompass those of the other two circles, since when we focus on the good of all we can trust that our own needs and those of our group will also be met. Thus when we move into a third-circle orientation, we do not lose our concern for first- and second-circle instincts. This point was brought home to a former colleague of mine, a philosophy professor. When his sons were about seven and eight, he took them and a neighbor boy fishing. As they were approaching shore at the end of the day, their boat overturned. He told me later, "I wasn't sure I could save them all, and instinctively I chose to save my own kids first." He was distraught, wondering about his own moral maturity and capacity to be concerned for the well-being of all. But his response simply reveals our normal human instinct to save "our own" first, and the fact that he questioned the ethics of this instinct reflects his additional motivation to act for the common good of all three boys. A third-circle orientation offers a certain freedom: we can attend to our self-interests without being limited by them, and we can care about clan and kin without being bound by them.

Living according to third-circle orientation does not require people to give up interest in their own well-being or the good of their group. It is just a wiser way to the same end.

The political philosopher Alexis de Tocqueville termed this stance "self-interest rightly understood"—often referred to as enlightened self-interest. De Tocqueville, a French aristocrat who visited the United States in 1831 to observe its still-young experiment in democracy, commented that the people he met "are fond of explaining almost all the actions of their lives by the principle of self-interest rightly understood; they show with complacency how an enlightened regard for themselves constantly prompts them to assist one another and inclines them willingly to sacrifice a portion of their time and property to the welfare of the state."[6] For de Tocqueville, self-interest rightly understood was an affirmative answer to a long-standing philosophical question: Is it advantageous to a person to work for the good of all?

Enlightened self-interest is often both the most principled and the most prudent choice for members of a group who must rely on one another for survival. This is illustrated by a story my colleague Sharon Daloz Parks once told. Her great-grandparents helped establish a new township in Nebraska in the latter half of the 1800s. Her forebearers and the other forty families lived in "soddies"—cold, dark, damp sod homes—for two years, until two community structures, the church and the school, were completed. Then they constructed their own permanent homes. These early settlers were fully aware of the limits of their resources, including time constraints, to build structures before the first winter. By investing in the town's first common structures, they were investing in their own long-term success and happiness. They knew having a church and school would strengthen their community by providing places to gather and to educate their children, as well as attract other settlers and thus help their young town to grow and prosper.

Third-circle orientation can also inform cultural traditions. In cultures the world over we find traditions rooted in principled reasoning that encourage people to make third-circle choices, trusting that their first- and second-circle concerns will be met when all benefit.

For example, in the Jewish tradition the ancient practice of the Grand Sabbath—the fiftieth year, the year of Jubilee based on lessons in the Pentateuch, the first five books of the Hebrew scriptures—marked a year of rest for people, animals, and the land, during which the ancient Jews engaged in profoundly principled acts. All people who through financial debt had fallen into indentured servitude were released, and all property lost through economic hardship was returned to the original owners.

Similarly, Native American tribes of the Pacific Northwest practice potlatch, a ceremony whose main purpose is the redistribution of wealth. On special occasions, such as births, weddings, and funerals, a hereditary leader gives away resources acquired by the family. A family's status is raised not by how much wealth they have but by how much they can give away.[7]

Further, barn raisings, still practiced today in Amish communities in the eastern United States and Canada, are communal acts of cooperation and reciprocity. Since barns are too massive to build alone, communities work together to accomplish this huge task in a single day. Although individual barn raisings primarily benefit a single member, the cooperative efforts also benefit the social fabric of the communities.

In addition, the pan-African ethic of *ubuntu*, which means "I am what I am because of who we all are,"[8] points to interconnectedness as the essence of being human. According to Desmond Tutu, former Anglican Archbishop of Capetown, South Africa: "You can't be human all by yourself, and when you have this quality, Ubuntu, you are known for your generosity. We think of ourselves far too frequently as just individuals, separated from one another, whereas you are connected and what you do affects the whole world. When you do well, it spreads out; it is for the whole of humanity."[9]

The common good worldview, like these social traditions, is an invitation to live not in isolation but in community. When asked "For whom do you labor?" people oriented to the us–them worldview answer, "For me, and for my kin," while people oriented to the common good worldview answer, "For the good of all."

"AM I IN THE THIRD CIRCLE?"

How can we know for sure when our choices and actions are for the common good and when they are not? The concept of the third circle offers a means for tethering the common good worldview to real-world practical action in the form of a simple question: "Am I in the third circle?" Implied in this question are several others:

> "Are the choices I am making grounded in principle?"
> "Am I attending to justice and to care?"
> "Whose concerns and interests have I diminished or ignored?"
> "What would it mean to recommit to the good of all concerned?"

The question "Am I in the third circle?" invites individuals to reflect on their choices and thus offers a tool to check orientation and intention. As humans, we naturally stray from making the most principled choices or considering what is good for everyone—we forget, take shortcuts, and yield to first- and second-circle concerns. We have the capacity, however, to observe ourselves and learn from such observations. Leadership educator Ron Heifetz describes reflection as the ability to place yourself in the balcony, as it were, and watch yourself while simultaneously dancing on the dance floor.[10] By standing back and observing ourselves, our organization, our community, or our nation, we can tell which of the three circles is informing the choice-making.

Reflection on our actions can open the door to judgments— what is good and bad, what is moral or immoral. But instead of judging ourselves, we can search for creative feedback and assessment of whether we're on course and make adjustments if we are not.

Reflection can also be a source of authenticity. When I am about to protest the harmful policies and practices of my department or the school board, if I remember that I also make mistakes, an element of honesty and humility enters into my protest, which ironically empowers it, causing me to speak from a place of authenticity.

This work is not about perfection; it is about persistence, trusting that periodic reflection leads to steady development. A person may have fifteen years' experience as a school superintendent. If reflection was not part if it, however, the total may actually amount to fifteen one-year experiences since the person did not optimize the position as a chance to learn and grow.

To initiate such reflection, we can ask, "Am I in the third circle?" once a week or even once a day. Then eventually it will become part of our thought processes, like a mantra of sorts. It's a worthwhile discipline in which to engage and clarify your intentions, especially before launching into some significant action. It's also useful to ask the question after taking action. Following a key meeting or at the end of the day, we can ask it to assess our actions to find out if they exhibited principled choice-making as well as concern for everyone involved.

Finally, we can observe our intentions in the moment in order to make more principled choices. For example, we may be engaged with a client and realize that something we just said did not reflect third-circle principles. At that instant, we can take a deep breath, ask "Am I in the third circle?" and alter our perspective to make a choice for the good of all.

By consciously operating from the perspective of the third circle, our choices and actions will naturally direct us and those around us toward the day when the common good becomes the prevailing worldview.

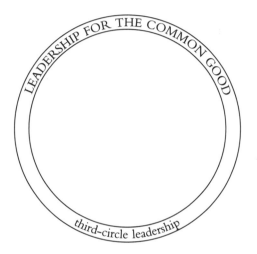
LEADERSHIP FOR THE COMMON GOOD

third–circle leadership

3 Reframing Leadership

HUMANITY WILL NOT ARRIVE at a future marked by a common good worldview by accident. Nor can we afford to wait for the slow-turning wheels of social evolution to carry us there. We need to move toward a common good worldview soon, given the problems we currently face. The earth cannot long survive ecological mistreatment due to the use of toxins. The threat of dirty bombs falling into the hands of terrorists makes any place on the planet vulnerable to a horrific act of hatred. The poor of the world, tired of getting the short end of the stick, are becoming increasingly impatient for social justice.

Our predicament demands the urgent intervention of leadership for the common good. Leadership is the ability to inspire a group to move freely with clarity and purpose in a new direction. Leadership can shake us out of our propensity for sleepwalking and challenge us to look at the difficult truths of the day. Leadership can also encourage us to believe that the important action required for change is possible.

Effective leadership is grounded in experience with the goal the group is moving toward. In some cases, a leader's experience is direct. A friend of mine who leads climbs up Mount Rainier in Washington knows the terrain well, and because his presence radiates this fact, people trust him to lead them up the mountain. In other cases, a leader's experience may be indirect, such as having researched the information associated with a goal. In still other cases, a leader's experience may derive from an intuition or vision of how to reach a goal. In all these cases, the leader has a glimpse of what others cannot yet see.

A leader's primary qualification for helping humanity move toward a future characterized by a common good worldview is experience in the moral territory of the third circle. Just as a pilot cannot fly a plane unless he is in the cockpit, it is not possible to further the common good without having a third-circle perspective. Leadership based on third-circle orientation provides the moral framework that makes leadership for the common good possible. In third-circle leadership a conscious concern for the good of all is added to principled leadership, resulting in a powerful moral force capable of advancing change for the common good.

INCORPORATING THE BEST OF EXISTING LEADERSHIP MODELS

Leadership for the common good, which is intended to advance change, draws on the best of the three basic types of leadership discussed since the 1980s: transformational leadership and transforming leadership, which offer two distinct approaches to social change, and transactional leadership, which provides the managerial know-how to effect change.

Transformational leadership recognizes that systems and structures of society are constructs, not fixed entities, and that new times require new systems and structures. Because most current systems and structures are by-products of the us-them worldview, which the common good worldview is meant to replace, transformational leadership, with its commitment to foundational change, lies at the heart of leadership for the common good. Transformational leaders ask such questions as: Are the programs, practices, and policies of this organization in the third circle? If not, what must change for the organization to be there?

Transforming leadership, on the other hand, seeks to transform not institutions and systems directly but rather the hearts and minds of those who created and now maintain and benefit from them. Transforming leaders want to improve the behavior of individuals to reflect increased moral maturity and motivation. As the hearts and minds of individuals are changed, the institutions in which they live and work also change. Transforming leadership is operating when a leader encourages people to ask themselves the question: Am I in the third circle?

Transformational and transforming leadership are most effective when applied together. Transforming leadership without a transformational agenda results in inspired people but no social change. For example, the green movement has inspired people nationwide to sort trash and recycle. In my travels around the country, however, I find that many airports and communities have not yet created systems to funnel that inspiration into action.

On the other hand, acts of transformational leadership may change the system, but if the hearts and minds of those who participate in the new system are not also changed, injustice will appear again in a new form. For example, the Emancipation Proclamation, signed into law in 1862, was not enough to change the hearts and minds of Americans regarding racism. Thus, despite the law, the black experience in America remains a long history of oppression that has taken new forms from generation to generation, from the KKK and Jim Crow laws to racial profiling and other forms of institutionalized bias.

When the strategies of transformational and transforming leadership are used in tandem, they work like rocket fuel, providing the propulsion necessary to overcome resistance of the status quo and advance far-reaching change for the common good. Here they are aided by the managerial wisdom of transactional leadership.

Transactional leadership is focused on the exchange between a leader and her followers and on keeping organizational wheels running smoothly. This gets things done. Managing functional details, however, often leads to an investment in preserving the status quo, even at the risk of losing sight of larger, moral questions at hand. As a result, it is possible to be a high-performing transactional leader within an unjust, immoral system. For instance, during the Nazi regime transactional matters were handled effectively—the trains ran on time, the gas chambers were managed with precision—but horror resulted. Yet, since change occurs more effectively when the details are managed well, transactional leadership is often of great value when it supports a noble goal.

An example of these three types of leadership working together is the anti-smoking movement in the United States. Marketing campaigns publicizing the dangers of smoking used transforming leadership strategies to change the hearts and minds of the public. Once the public will for change was ignited, transformational leadership strategies brought about federal laws establishing smoke-free standards in workplaces, public spaces, and even restaurants and bars. Transactional leadership techniques kept this movement organized, allowing for steady progress despite the tobacco industry's extensive lobbying efforts to halt the change.

THE FOUR CORNERSTONES OF LEADERSHIP FOR THE COMMON GOOD

When the third-circle orientation is brought to bear upon the best of these three types of leadership, leadership aligns with its highest purpose—to lead us into a future in which every corner of the earth is a place where life can prosper. Leadership aligned with its highest purpose and focused on the common good is based on four foundational principles, or cornerstones. This marriage of purpose and foundational principles equips leadership to address the most difficult challenges of the day to advance the common good.

Three of the four cornerstones are basic principles of the third circle: care, justice, and inclusiveness. The fourth, moral urgency, reflects the ethical obligation to eliminate suffering as quickly as possible anytime and anywhere it occurs.

Care: The Practice of Stewardship

The first cornerstone of leadership for the common good is care. Within the third circle, care becomes a concern for all life and the systems that support it. When influenced by care, leadership takes on the characteristics of stewardship. A steward is someone who cares for a household, assets, or other resources owned by someone else, often in the owner's absence, out of a sense of duty and commitment to care.

When leadership is cast as stewardship of the common good, then two questions arise: Who is the owner? and How extensive is the household? The question of ownership can be answered either philosophically or theologically. From a philosophical standpoint, the owner is all people, including those not yet born. From this point of view, stewardship means attending to the legacy our generation leaves behind for the children of the future.

Similarly, the Great Law of the Iroquois Confederacy urges those living today to consider the impact of their choices on the next seven generations. It is in this spirit that stewards plant shade trees under which they will never sit, dig wells from which others will drink, light fires that will warm strangers they may never meet. From a theological point of view, the owner is Spirit and stewards act in accord with the intentions of Spirit, guided by divine qualities such as love, generosity, and compassion.

The household that such stewards for the common good care for is both local and global. In this respect, stewardship for the common good means safeguarding the earth and advocating for the inalienable rights of people everywhere. This includes caring about the destruction of rainforests in Brazil, nuclear accidents in Chernobyl, Russia, and northeastern Japan, and air pollution in China because such crises affect the life-giving systems that support us all, regardless of national borders. Yet stewardship for the common good also focuses on local concerns, albeit in a global context, as leaders exercise care for resources and people in their own corners of the world, including in neighborhoods, institutions, and corporations.

Leadership as stewardship can be modeled and learned, as evidenced in the story of Jim David, a friend of mine. Jim's reputation for stewardship in the corporate sector has its origins in his first week as an employee at a major corporation in Seattle. While attending a training course in California, he heard the news that his father, back in Seattle, had suddenly been hospitalized and was deathly ill. His instincts kicked in, and he flew home that evening without taking time to alert his new boss, who was at the training with him. Early the next morning, while Jim was at home preparing to see his father, Jim's new boss, who had also flown home the previous evening, paid him a visit. Jim began to excuse his behavior, when his boss said, "Jim, I heard about your father's illness and tried to get here as soon as I could. Is there anything the company can do? We're prepared to fly your father to the Mayo Clinic in Rochester, Minnesota, or do whatever is necessary to get him the best care possible. We value family, and I am here to let you know that the company stands behind you. For now, do whatever you need to for your family. Your job at the company is secure."

Later that week, at his father's funeral, Jim was profoundly touched to see every manager from the Seattle office in attendance. He was stunned by the care the company's core leadership team expressed and never forgot it. Subsequently, he became known in the corporate world for demonstrating leadership according to the same principle of care and has inspired many others to lead this way as well.

A steward of the common good acts in the present to take care of the current needs of people and resources, yet is also committed to acting on behalf of future generations just as a steward of a fortune is paid to see that the fortune grows through the years. A remarkable story of stewardship of a preferred future comes from New College, Oxford. In the 1950s, the College Council learned that the five-hundred-year-old oak beams in the ceiling of the dining hall had become infested with beetles and needed replacing. A young faculty member suggested that the college dean meet with the local forester, who took the dean for a walk in the woods, pointed to a grove of oaks, and said, "There are the timbers you will need for the hall. When oak trees were harvested for New College, the architect assumed they would last five hundred years, so he directed the forester at the time to plant a grove of one hundred oak saplings. Since that day, twenty generations of foresters have tended these trees."

Stewardship for the common good does not necessarily require thinking ahead five hundred years, but it does mean looking beyond ourselves and our own generation to become caregivers on behalf of people we will never meet and a future we will never see.

Justice: The Exercise of Equality and Equity

The second cornerstone of leadership for the common good is justice. Justice involves the creation of laws, policies, systems, and institutions that operate for the common good in practical ways. Justice is, in large part, care crystallized in social constructs, just as care is the motivator of justice.

Fundamental to the concept of justice is the notion of equality—in Francis Bellamy's words, "justice for all." Bellamy wrote the Pledge of Allegiance at the end of the nineteenth century, after the Emancipation Proclamation had passed and just as the women's suffrage movement was gaining strength. Being a progressive theologian, he very likely thought of women and blacks as he wrote the word *all*. In the hundred years since then, the meaning of *all* has been expanded through other social agendas, such as the Person with Disabilities Act and the Twenty-Sixth Amendment to the Constitution, which gave eighteen-year-olds the right to vote.

Today, despite such social progress, many people still fall outside the realm in which justice operates in the United States. Injustice lingers as long as existing systems and structures continue to foster privilege for some and deprivation for others. As Martin Luther King Jr. pointed out in his Letter from a Birmingham Jail, "Injustice anywhere is a threat to justice everywhere."[1] Injustice not only hurts the least fortunate and most vulnerable; it also undermines the moral character of the privileged who are aware of it yet do nothing about it.

Until justice is truly available to all, I suggest that Bellamy's phrase "justice for all" be amended to include the phrase "and an additional measure of mercy for the least fortunate and most vulnerable." A society's greatness is determined not by how well its elite fare but by the degree of compassion extended to those who, by chance of birth or circumstances, have insufficient resources to live a decent life. Thus one of the essential tasks of leadership for the common good is attending to the inequities in any given situation and transforming the related systems and structures, policies and institutions so they reflect social justice.

For this reason, the path to justice for all is not always by way of equality alone. Consider, for example, the distribution of restrooms at a theater. As men and women head for the restrooms at intermission, the lines to the women's restrooms are almost always much longer. When designing the building, the architects, no doubt thinking of equality, planned four restrooms for men and four for women. But this does not address the real needs of the people involved. To offer genuine equality, the theater owners would need to convert perhaps two of the men's restrooms to serve the needs of women.

Similarly, public schools in the United States were integrated in an effort to offer equal opportunities to all students, yet academic achievement and graduation rates among African Americans and Hispanics remain significantly lower than among their white counterparts. Although the children and their families are partially responsible, many institutional biases in the school systems undermine the success of minority youth. In such circumstances, something more than equality is needed.

Equity, which expands the work of justice beyond equality by transforming systems and structures to support true justice, levels the unequal playing field of many societal situations. We expect umpires to interpret the rules fairly for both sports teams competing in a game, and when they don't fans protest. What if the umpire and even the playing field have a built-in bias for the home team? That is, what if the game is rigged? Equity makes the game fair by creating structural and behavioral changes that level the playing field. At first, changes are likely to feel unfair to members of the home team, who are used to the game as they have known it. Equity often appears in the eyes of the privileged as unfair. For example, they wonder why academic coaches should be hired by school districts to mentor promising students in inner-city schools and be paid for by their tax dollars. Once the playing field is level, fairness and equality alone will serve to maintain the common good. But until then, equity is needed to assure justice.

An example of the value of social equity agendas is the United States law known as Title IX, enacted in 1972, which states: "No person in the United States shall, on the basis of sex, be excluded from participation in, be denied benefits of, or be subject to discrimination under any education program or activity receiving Federal assistance."[2] The net result of this act on justice has been profound. In 1972, only 7 percent of law degrees and 9 percent of medical degrees were earned by women. By 2007, those percentages increased to 47 and 43, respectively. In that same period, the picture of college athletics changed just as dramatically. A total of 3,715 women's athletics teams were added to the intercollegiate sports scene, and the number of women athletes grew from 32,000 to 165,000.[3]

Besides being principled, equity is also prudent. Those who are disadvantaged will not be content forever, and discontent breeds destructive behavior, ultimately affecting the advantaged as well, although they may not be conscious of this potential. I am reminded of a political cartoon depicting people on a large boat. Those at one end of the boat, dressed in tuxedos and gowns, are drinking champagne and enjoying good food, while those at the other end are dressed in old clothes and look sad, and one young man with a gun is shooting holes in the boat's bottom, causing water to seep in. The caption, a remark by one of the men on the opulent side, reads, "Will you look at that fool shooting holes in his end of the boat!" Considering our common life as one human family, the unfair distribution of resources, leaving some of our sisters and brothers vulnerable, can impact us all.

Today, despite the inspiring words of the Pledge of Allegiance, children born in poverty, women, and minorities of all kinds still remain disadvantaged in the United States. Globally, the people of Darfur, Chad, Myanmar, and other undeveloped countries still struggle for daily bread, while many of us in developed nations enjoy daily luxuries like lattes, movies, and golf. Our current work is to commit to leveling the global playing field level through courageous laws, institutions, and policies that provide equity and justice.

Inclusiveness: Bringing All into the Circle

The third cornerstone of leadership for the common good is inclusiveness, which extends the leader's concern for the effects of his choices beyond clan and kin to everyone influenced by those choices. It means making sure that all people in a given family, neighborhood,

institution, or other community have equitable access to power, priv-
ileges, and resources in the system and thus can flourish. Inclusiveness
can also entail attention to the well-being of nonhuman communities,
such as other species, as well as to the environment—the water, air,
earth—within the leader's scope of concern.

An example of an organization whose leadership puts inclusiveness front and center is Medecins Sans Frontieres (MSF),
known in the United States and Canada as Doctors Without Borders. Founded in France by journalists and doctors in 1971 and
committed to the idea that no one should be denied medical attention, this global humanitarian organization provides assistance
especially in places around the world where people's survival is
threatened by war, epidemics, or natural disasters, also advocating
for the just administration of aid systems and medical protocols in
such situations. Its Web site states: "MSF's work is based on the
humanitarian principles of medical ethics and impartiality. The
organization is committed to bringing quality medical care to
people caught in crisis regardless of race, religion, or political affiliation."[4]

This third cornerstone of leadership for the common good
may require an extra measure of attention compared with the others. We know when our choices are principled or unprincipled,
when they reflect care or justice and when they do not, as our
moral sensibilities give us this information. But shifting our orientation from our own needs or a group's conventions to concern for
all calls for a willingness to question our conscious and unconscious
biases or prejudices. To consider a wide range of perspectives and
make choices that benefit all who are affected by them, it can be
helpful to reflect on the following questions:

- In what way might my definition of all be limited?
- Who tends to receive favored treatment in my
  community?

- Who experiences exclusion, whether obvious or subtle, from the benefits and social networks of my community?

Inclusiveness also means incorporating multiple viewpoints in the decision-making process. To reach a solution beneficial for the common good, it is important that representatives of various interest groups, including opposition parties, provide information about their needs and views. This means listening to people with minority points of view, trusting that each offers a unique perspective capable of enriching the change process. Although this means of developing multicultural competence can seem daunting at the outset, it yields worthwhile results. We can never know who might offer the key idea that unlocks the door to a solution.

Leaders for the common good who seek social change can anticipate resistance. Some people may dismiss a leader's vision as unrealistic, while others may endlessly debate issues, delaying actions that might lead to change, or oppose change and champion the status quo due to fear of the unknown. A principled response to resistance is to invite the resistance to join. In his poem "Outwitted," Edwin Markham makes this point beautifully:

He drew a circle that shut me out—
Heretic, rebel, a thing to flout.
But Love and I had the wit to win:
We drew a circle that took him in![5]

Such radical inclusiveness poses the greatest risk because it means welcoming those who could do harm to the change process. Yet diverse people finding a way forward together also offers the greatest transformation potential for everyone involved. Handled with graciousness and courage, such an expression of inclusiveness creates a challenging but powerful context for change.

In this regard, leadership for the common good is consonant with the spirit of nonviolence. The nonviolent approach is to confront injustice by inviting its perpetrators to become transformed through an encounter with love seeking justice. This is why we see so many leaders who have worked to advance the common good turning to the principles of nonviolence.

Moral Urgency: The Importance of When

The fourth cornerstone of leadership for the common good is moral urgency, a response to the need for timely change. At present, we don't have the luxury of taking baby steps toward a new common good worldview. Martin Luther King Jr.'s words spoken in 1967 are still relevant today: "We are confronted with the fierce urgency of now. In this unfolding conundrum of life and history, there is such a thing as being too late."[6]

Every change-producing strategy is a blend of methodology and timing—of how and when change will occur. Of the two, making the plan is usually easier than taking action. For this reason, focusing unduly on *how* a change will happen can become a delay tactic. To make sure a change occurs, a leader needs to stay focused on *when* it can occur.

Large complex social problems can be solved more quickly than we think when moral urgency becomes the catalyst for change. For example, in 1993 when Patrus Ananias became mayor of Belo Horizonte, the fourth largest city in Brazil, he was outraged by the level of hunger suffered by the poor. His sense of moral urgency helped him quickly reduce hunger. In his first month as mayor, he called on his staff and other community leaders to act with exigency on behalf of the hungry, declaring that from that time forward access to food in his city would be a right of citizenship. The long-term result of his declaration is that the child mortality and malnutrition rates, considered measures of hunger in a population, have since decreased by 60 percent and 75 percent respectively.[7]

Having a deadline, especially when people's lives are at stake, can also hasten solutions to problems by stimulating increased creativity. For instance, the scientists and engineers who brought the crew of *Apollo 13* safely back to earth operated with strong passion and unusual innovation because the two leaders—James A. Lovell Jr., commander of *Apollo 13*, and "Gene" Kranz, NASA flight director—focused the entire team's attention on solving a key problem in a short time frame with limited resources. The ground engineers had thirty-six hours to improvise a repair to the air filtration system using only the supplies the astronauts had on hand. Lovell later wrote: "The contraption wasn't very handsome, but it worked."[8]

A CALL FOR LEADERS FOR THE COMMON GOOD

The shift necessary to move from today's us-them worldview to the common good worldview will require the efforts of leaders in all sectors of society. Not only are all welcome as leaders for the common good but the moral urgency to improve world conditions means that all are needed, including national and international positional leaders. One stellar example of such a leader continues to be Anwar Sadat, president of Egypt from 1970 to 1981. In a speech to the Egyptian parliament in 1977, Sadat affirmed his desire to go to the Israeli Knesset to negotiate peace with the Israelis. Sadat's speech there initiated a new momentum for peace that culminated in the 1978 Camp David Accords and a peace treaty between Egypt and Israel in 1979.

Other positional leaders for the common good work at the regional or city level of government, or in institutions, corporations, or other organizations. An example of such leadership at this level is the Champlain Initiative, a regional organization in Chittenden County, Vermont, founded in 1996 and sustained by the leadership of four women: Martha Maksym, Penrose Jackson, Gretchen

Morse, and Beth Kuhn. The initiative draws people from all sectors to work together for the physical, spiritual, economic, social, and cultural vitality of the region.

Positional leaders for the common good often receive recognition for what they do, while other citizens tend to defer to them. Assuming that a leader for the common good is better known or more powerfully positioned than they are, they wait for a Gandhi, a Martin Luther King Jr., or a Rachel Carson. But in fact anyone can decide to take principled action that benefits everyone involved, becoming what I call an "everyday leader for the common good."

Perhaps the quintessential example of an everyday leader for the common good is Rosa Parks, the black seamstress who on her way home one December evening in 1955, her arms full of groceries, refused to get up from her seat on a Montgomery, Alabama, bus so a white man could sit. Her arrest sparked the Montgomery bus boycott and launched the Civil Rights Movement.

Rosa Parks was no stranger to political activism, having served in the state and local NAACP chapters for over ten years and having attended a two-week training program at Myles Horton's Highlander Folk School designed to empower grassroots leaders to work for racial equality. But even given her background, it would not have been possible to predict that she would catalyze such social change.

Everyday leadership for the common good does not require the kind of training Rosa Parks had. A single principled act by anyone holds the potential for creating a ripple effect of significant change. For example, it was a custodian at the Watergate Hotel, Frank Wills, who one day in June 1972 discovered tape on the door of the Democratic Headquarters office, recorded the break-in in the security log, and called the police, performing his job with such attention and integrity that it led to the Watergate scandal and ultimately to the resignation of President Nixon.

Similarly, the actions of a housewife from Northern Ireland, Betty Williams, precipitated the longest cessation of violence known in that part of the world. In August of 1976, after witnessing the death of innocent bystanders during the ongoing Catholic-Protestant conflict in the streets of Belfast, Ireland, she went door to door imploring her neighbors to help stop the violence. Remarkably, her efforts were met with great enthusiasm, particularly by Mairead Corrigan, the aunt of children who had been killed. The two women led a campaign for peace in Northern Ireland that eventually involved tens of thousands of people and were awarded the Nobel Peace Prize in 1977.

Anywhere, anytime, there are opportunities for ordinary citizens to engage in leadership for the common good. Any mother could ask, "What can I do at my daughter's school today that will improve the educational experience for all of the children?" Any schoolchild can decide to inspire his peers to donate their nickels, dimes, and quarters over the course of a year to fund the digging of a well in Africa. And when ordinary people participate in endeavors for the common good, it can not only change them personally but also bring change in their corner of the world. Those who have volunteered to help fill sandbags to stop a river from flooding a town or contributed foodstuffs to a food drive or been part of a cleanup team at a park know firsthand how such experiences can be personally rewarding and also build community, the sense among participants that all people are of one family and have common interests and goals.

It's not possible to prejudge how large or small an individual's contribution might be to the shift to a common good worldview. The key is to conduct our lives according to a third-circle orientation. When we commit ourselves to third-circle living, we may be surprised at where it will take us and what changes we can catalyze. And whether we become a positional leader or not, whether our actions become well known or not, we'll be happier people as a result of fostering the common good in our corner of the world.

Part II

THE SEVEN COMMON GOOD
LEADERSHIP PRACTICES

IF THE QUESTION "Am I in the third circle?" provides the leader with a compass, the seven common good leadership practices are the leader's roadmap. As the outer circle of the leadership model suggests, the common good is the goal. We get there by engaging the seven common good leadership practices arranged within the circle. These seven practices can be done separately, but they also build on each other when performed progressively in clockwise order around the model, strengthening a leader's capacity to advance the common good.

The three Vs (values, vision, and voice), found where the corners of the triangle touch the circle, represent internal capacity building, which helps leaders become clear about their identity and vocation. The three arcs in the model house three concepts that describe external elements which leaders are responsible for either engaging or cocreating. These external elements help establish the setting and climate within which progress for the common good is best pursued.

Courage is at the center of the model, since it both fuels and draws from the other six practices. Courage invigorates the entire process of leadership for the common good, making it a powerful means of social transformation.

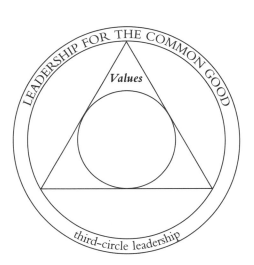

4 Choosing Your Personal Values

NELSON MANDELA was born into the royal family of the Thembu people in the Transkei region of South Africa and raised to follow in his father's footsteps as a high officer among the Thembu, but his contribution to the well-being of his people took a different path. As a young man he traveled to Johannesburg, where he found a job in a law office and entered law school. He also joined the African National Congress (ANC) in 1944 and took a leadership role in its powerful Youth League.

When the pro-apartheid National Party won the national election in 1948, Mandela left law school to devote himself fully to politics. He helped lead the ANC's 1952 passive resistance movement against apartheid. He was also instrumental in developing the Freedom Charter, which became the foundation of the anti-apartheid movement.

In 1962, Mandela, who by this time was regarded as the most influential black leader in South Africa and a potent symbol of resistance to apartheid, was arrested by the South African military police. In 1964, the government pressed further charges against him, including conspiracy to overthrow the government, sabotage, and high treason.

In his defense statement at the April 1964 trial, Mandela spoke of his ancestors' greatness as fighters for the freedom of their people and how their heroism had inspired his own efforts for freedom and justice:

> *In my youth in the Transkei, I listened to the elders of my tribe telling stories of the old days. Amongst the tales they related to me were those of wars fought by our ancestors in defence of the fatherland . . . I hoped then that life might offer me the opportunity to serve my people and make my own humble contribution to their freedom struggle. This is what has motivated me in all that I have done in relation to the charges made against me in this case.*[1]

He closed his statement by declaring the values that had guided his choices over the span of two decades:

> *I have fought against white domination, and I have fought against black domination. I have cherished the ideal of a democratic and free society in which all persons live together in harmony and with equal opportunities. It is an ideal which I hope to live for and to achieve. But if needs be, it is an ideal for which I am prepared to die.*[2]

Mandela spent the next twenty-six years in prison. The other political prisoners looked to him as a source of courage and hope. Outside the prison walls, he was still widely regarded as a potent symbol of resistance to apartheid.

Mandela, along with other ANC leaders, was finally released from prison in 1990, when South African President F. W. de Klerk reversed the ban on the ANC in one of the early steps toward ending apartheid. During his first speech after his release, Mandela repeated the exact words with which he had ended his defense statement in 1964—reiterating his values of freedom, justice, and harmony, as well as his willingness to die fighting to realize these principles, letting it be known that nearly three decades in prison had not diminished but rather increased his commitment to his values.

He continued to draw upon these values as he moved into a new level of leadership in his country. On May 10, 1994, Mandela was inaugurated as the first democratically elected president of South Africa. In his inaugural address, he once again spoke of the values of freedom, justice, and harmony:

> *We understand it still that there is no easy road to freedom. We know it well that none of us acting alone can achieve success. We must therefore act together as a united people, for national reconciliation, for nation building, for the birth of a new world. Let there be justice for all. Let there be peace for all. Let there be work, bread, water, and salt for all. Let each know that for each the body, the mind, and the soul have been freed to fulfill themselves.*[3]

Nelson Mandela is a leader who exemplifies the importance of choosing personal values and using them to work for change.

Personal values are the foundation upon which leadership for the common good rests, as Nelson Mandela's life suggests. Values are not just philosophical ideals; they are tangible moral assets meant to be chosen, prized, and put into action.

Once they are chosen by individuals, values become personal guidelines for making choices. Everyone has only twenty-four hours in a day and limited energy and resources, so we cannot do and have everything but must prioritize and make choices with the help of personal values. When our choices are grounded in what matters, we can live with the consequences of those choices as well as more readily perceive their benefits.

For example, a father who chooses to leave behind a high-paying career to spend more time with his children may sometimes wonder, "If I had kept that job, we might have been able to go on more exciting vacations, the children might have been able to enroll in a better college, or they could have become more independent." As such nagging thoughts arise, this father can be comforted knowing that he made his decision based on his personal values, live with the consequences, and also perceive its benefits while seeing his children grow up and making it to all of the teacher conferences, recitals, and athletic events.

To yield their best gifts, personal values need to be prized. When people prize personal values, they deepen their commitment to them and allow them to shape their behavior and catalyze their actions. Because Rosa Parks prized the value of racial equality, she stayed seated on the bus in Montgomery, Alabama, stoking the Civil Rights Movement. Similarly, because Mother Teresa prized the value of compassion, she cared for the dying in Calcutta, India. These are both famous people, but examples of cherishing personal values can be found everywhere among ordinary citizens. A working single mother who prizes the value of family comes home each evening to make dinner for her children and help them with their homework. A Methodist pastor who prizes the value of tolerance among religious traditions holds midweek interfaith services that include a Jewish rabbi, a Catholic priest, and a Muslim imam, even though some members of the congregation are hesitant.

When we prize our personal values, we not only act on them but do so repeatedly over time, both when it is easy and when it is hard. For instance, Nelson Mandela prized justice before he went to prison, advocated for justice while in prison, and stayed true to the value of justice when he became president. Some days his commitment to justice brought him acclaim and on other days hardship.

Further, when people prize personal values, their values give back to them in ways that enrich their lives. Those who commit to the value of wisdom over time find themselves becoming wiser. People who become standard-bearers for truth discover that truth slowly fills their hearts and minds and, albeit sometimes painfully, eventually sets them free. A person who pledges herself to the value of integrity will eventually lead an undivided life, behaving as the same honest person whether at work, at home, or in the community. Those who prize love often end up in situations where they are loved in return.

Groups, too, may use values as the foundation upon which they work for the common good. These values are expressed in mission statements, declarations, and project plans. However, despite the best of intentions, unless a group's values are derived from the personal values of its members, they lack staying power. In such cases, these values all too often devolve into platitudes posted on the break-room wall or kept in a three-ring binder on a shelf rather than catalyzing action for the common good.

Most individuals who commit to their personal values can also find the inner motivation to commit to a team effort. In the process, they discover how their values can serve as stepping stones to the values of the groups to which they belong. As a result, both individuals and groups are well served.

It is through our personal values that we establish a personal relationship with principles, which are the essence of third-circle orientation. The range of personal values is greater than the range of principles. Principles are moral reference points that guide and direct people toward choices advancing the good of all. Personal values, on the other hand, can align with a first-, second-, or third-circle interest. They can be self oriented, social oriented, or principle oriented.

Consider, for example, how the business value of making a profit is viewed differently by individuals with these three orientations. Business leaders whose values are self-oriented are focused on the acquisition of power and resources for their own gain and can become motivated by greed. In the movie *Wall Street*, the character Gordon Gecko expresses the values of a self-absorbed business leader intent only on personal profit in his well-known line "Greed is good."

A CEO whose values are social oriented might prioritize stock prices, since it benefits his primary peer groups—board members and stockholders—while dismissing as less important the effect his choices might have on other stakeholders in a company, including the employees, the customers, the community, and the environment.

Business leaders whose values are principle oriented look beyond the interest of self and group. They are naturally drawn to the triple-bottom-line concept of measuring success by social and ecological as well as economic standards, known as "people, planet, and profit." Thus they balance concerns for profit with attention to the interests of workers, customers, and investors, as well as to the company's ecological footprint. The principled orientation of such leaders, expressed through their values, prompts them to act according to a broad third-circle commitment to the common good.

Only principle-oriented values can promote the common good. Thus throughout this book, wherever the term "values" is used unqualified, it refers to principle-oriented values.

VALUES-BASED LEADERSHIP

Values are the taproot for all forms of leadership and especially leadership for the common good. Values provide leaders with a stable center from which to act and help them retain steadiness and moral clarity in times of challenge.

One of the clearest demonstrations I have seen of the benefits of having a stable center was enacted by an Aikido master. The master held a wooden sword aloft in one hand and instructed a student to attempt to strike him using an overhead blow with another sword. Each time, the disciple's sword glanced off the master's sword without touching him. Throughout, the master continued to talk about the effectiveness of knowing how to function from one's physical and spiritual center.

Values center us in the same way, offering us an internal compass with which to navigate choices. By examining the options in any given moment in light of personal values, leaders can choose actions that honor those core values even while facing severe challenges. Leaders who have cultivated a relationship with their core values are able to do what they know is right even when it is unpopular, such as when the way forward is clear from a moral standpoint but might seem potentially costly from an economic or political perspective.

For example, Aaron Feuerstein, owner and CEO of Malden Mills, the textile plant that invented Polartec fabric, relied on his personal values in an emergency situation for his business. When the plant, which was located in the small city of Lawrence, Massachusetts, burned to the ground on December 11, 1995, Feuerstein made a series of magnanimous decisions that surprised everyone. Although colleagues encouraged him to move the plant to the South or overseas, where he could pay lower wages, he decided instead to rebuild it on the same spot to save jobs. Moreover, only days after the fire he called a meeting of his workers and announced that for the next thirty days all employees would receive their full salary. Thirty days later he announced that he would extend workers' salaries at least another thirty days. In all, he paid out $25 million to his three thousand employees during the rebuilding period. Feuerstein later indicated that his decisions had been guided by his Jewish faith and his study of the Talmud, which says not to take advantage of the working man because he is poor and needy.[4] "I have a responsibility to the worker, both blue-collar and white-collar. I have an equal responsibility to the community. It would have been unconscionable to put 3,000 people on the streets and deliver a deathblow to the cities of Lawrence and Methuen,"[5] Feuerstein explained. When Morley Safer, reporter for the TV news program *60 Minutes*, asked Feuerstein if in retrospect he considered this a wise business decision, Feuerstein replied, "I think it was a wise business decision, but that is not why I did it. I did it because it was the right thing to do."[6]

Values can also clarify the purpose of what leaders are undertaking. In 1985, shortly after accepting a position at a Jesuit university, I was walking with a new colleague across campus when he introduced to me a member of the Jesuit community and explained that I was designing a new undergraduate leadership development program. The Jesuit father asked me without hesitation, "For what purpose?"

I responded, "To help students connect a sense of moral responsibility to their leadership."

He asked again, "For what purpose?"

Surprised, I thought quickly and replied, "So their leadership is informed by questions of depth and meaning."

He asked yet again, "For what purpose?"

With growing frustration, I answered, "So they can become creators of a more just society."

Then he smiled and said, "Good."

This man had pushed me until I finally articulated one of my personal values, justice, and linked it with the program. The conversation was unorthodox, yet it helped me launch a more clearly focused program. I had thought I was creating the program to serve the students, but after this conversation I understood its deeper purpose: to help them serve as coshapers of a more just society.

Finally, values-based leadership often creates a multiplier effect. As people witness the integrity and effectiveness of leadership based on a leader's personal values, they often want to emulate it. They are inspired to choose their personal core values and then commit to them in their own endeavors.

Whether individually or collectively, it takes courage and discipline to integrate our values into our daily lives. It is not easy to commit to acting from values such as love, integrity, or fairness. Yet as we practice aligning our daily choices with our personal values, whether facing major or minor decisions, we lead our lives with greater intention and increased integrity and peace of mind.

CHOOSING PERSONAL VALUES

Personal values must be intentionally and freely chosen. Otherwise, other forces in our lives may choose our values for us.

As children we passively absorb values from our social environment—parents, teachers, religion, and the broader popular culture. We carry these as unexamined assumptions about how life works or what constitutes a good one. Part of the maturation process is to examine these unconsciously held values and consciously choose the core values we will carry into adulthood. If we don't, then we are by default unconsciously acting according to others' values. Even if we inherit a noble value, such as honesty, until we consciously embrace it ourselves, it remains simply a moral sentiment.

Nelson Mandela actively chose his personal values. He stated in court in 1964 that when growing up he had not only heard the stories of his ancestors who had fought for freedom, but he chose to make his own "humble contribution to their freedom struggle."[7] In this way, he transformed his forebearers' commitment to freedom into a personal value in his own life.

Personal values must be chosen not only intentionally but also freely. Many people live a particular lifestyle, vote a certain way, or worship in a specific tradition because their parents did before them. Oppressive familial, social, or political systems can keep people from choosing values that are aligned with their authentic selves, as illustrated by a chance encounter I had with a fellow student on commencement day at my university. As we walked together across campus toward the ceremony site, I asked him, "Are you excited about graduating?" He replied, "No, not really." Knowing that he had been accepted at a dental school, I said "That's surprising, since you're on your way to becoming a dentist." Tears filled his eyes, and his hands shook as he blurted out, "I don't want to be a dentist. My father wants me to be a dentist."

There is nothing wrong with honoring a family tradition or emulating a good role model, but these actions are damaging when they result in individuals forfeiting their own personal values and visions. The litmus test is: did the person cross the threshold of commitment to a value by saying yes to the question "Is this how I intend to live my life, too?" If a person can't say no, her yes is not really a yes.

Moreover, a yes is not a real yes if the alternative options are false. My father-in-law was a young boy during World War II, when many items were rationed. Whenever he had an extra nickel, he rode his bike to the local soda fountain to buy an ice cream cone. Each time he would ask the store owner, "What kind of ice cream do you have today?" The owner would smile and say, "We have vanilla, white or plain. Which would you like?" Vanilla ice cream is good, but it is not a real choice if chocolate and strawberry are not also on the menu.

We see free choice-making among alternatives demonstrated in Nelson Mandela's life. For instance, in working for the dissolution of apartheid Nelson Mandela had the option of using violence. He had had experiences with fighting, having been a boxer in college, and was aware of ancestors who had been warriors. In addition, at one point Mandela was the commander-in-chief of a splinter group of the ANC, which, though generally committed to nonviolence and bringing an end to apartheid, founded a branch organization that engaged in sabotage and was preparing for guerrilla warfare.

During his 1964 trial, Mandela explained: "At the beginning of June 1961, after a long and anxious assessment of the South African situation, I, and some colleagues, came to the conclusion that as violence in this country was inevitable, it would be unrealistic and wrong for African leaders to continue preaching peace and nonviolence at a time when the government met our peaceful demands with force. . . . It was only when all else had failed, when all channels of peaceful protest had been barred to us, that the decision was made to embark on violent forms of political struggle."[8] Later, Mandela commented that this choice violated the ANC's own principles, yet at the time they could not see how else to proceed.[9] Despite this option of violence, however, Mandela eventually chose to follow in the footsteps of Gandhi and Martin Luther King Jr. and lead reform through nonviolent resistance, reflecting how he had selected this option freely from among others he had considered.

Personal values must also be chosen with awareness of their potential cost. Mandela's social activism was a powerful choice in part because he understood the cost. He knew that by continuing to rally the black population of South Africa to demand equal rights he would eventually be either jailed or killed. He realized, too, that his choices put his family in jeopardy, yet he and his wife, Winnie, decided together that the importance of the struggle for freedom outweighed the risks. In fact, Winnie Mandela continued the work to end apartheid while Nelson was in prison, even though during those years she received fifteen death threats and her house was bombed.

Choosing personal values does not always require individuals to stare death in the face, but it does necessitate consciousness of possible consequences. A person who values the dignity of all people might decide to ask a relative not to tell racist jokes, knowing that it could cause tension at the family reunion. A resident of a small town might choose to write a letter to the editor of the local newspaper on healthcare reform or immigration reform, realizing it might spark local rumors. Another individual, motivated by love, might opt to confront a buddy about his drinking habit, aware that it could jeopardize the friendship.

Some people question the usefulness of choosing personal values, suggesting it is usually an exercise in idealism, that the values people choose are more principled than the values by which they actually live. I contend, however, along with developmental theorists, that behavior is preceded by awareness and that aspiring to chosen values enhances principled choicemaking. When we focus on our values, we naturally strive to engage in principled behavior. By professing our values, even if at first we don't act on them consistently, we begin to integrate them into our behaviors.

Choosing personal values tends to bring people together as well. The personal values people hold are often the most universal. I have observed this repeatedly in a room of people who have just identified their personal values. When asked to stand as I name one of their values, the entire group is almost always standing after as few as eight values have been named.

It is sometimes pointed out that the same value may have different meanings for different people, and thus individuals with apparently the same values can potentially be in conflict with each other. This is especially true with a value such as family. For some people, the word *family* refers to the traditional nuclear family, while for others it connotes a global family and includes gay and lesbian families. It turns out, however, that conflict becomes less intimidating and more productive in the context of values. When people honor their personal values, such as love, truth, or justice, while in conflict with another, the conflict itself is often transformed. Simply having personal values becomes a common ground where individuals can meet with mutual respect.

Reflecting on our personal values allows us to adhere to them more often. Reflection does not result in a report card that indicates whether we did or did not act according to our core values on any given day. Rather, the discipline of reflection can change our psyche and behavior, helping us become more deeply rooted and more conscious of our habits.

When we are in close relationship with our core values, they are likely to call us into an internal dialogue that illuminates our motivations, much as the Jesuit did when he repeatedly asked me, "For what purpose?" We can ask ourselves, "What do my core values expect of me today?" then listen deeply to what our mind, heart, and spirit tell us to do. Knowing our core values also allows us to personalize the question "Am I in the third circle?" by transforming it into an inquiry about values, such as "Am I honoring my core values?" Just as the North Star can guide us geographically, a close relationship with our core values can indicate whether we are directing our actions toward the common good.

Reflecting on our core values and conducting inner dialogues about their implications is about persistence not perfection. An old Cherokee chief told his grandson: "A terrible fight is going on inside me. It is a fight between two wolves. One is evil—he is anger, envy, greed, arrogance, and ego. The other is good—he is joy, peace, love, hope, generosity, and truth. This same fight is going on inside you, and inside every other person, too."

The grandson thought about it for a minute and then asked, "Which wolf will win?"

The chief replied, "The one you feed."[10]

People who persist in reminding themselves of their core values will more quickly recognize when they are getting off track and then find their balance and redirect their efforts. The point is to notice the gap between what we profess and what we do, and try constantly to decrease it. This we can do through a daily habit of engaging with our values. Each day, we receive thousands of messages from popular culture—through commercials, billboards, and pop-up advertising on the Web—asking us to value things to which we may not want to be committed. In the face of that barrage of choices, a relationship with our core values helps us stay grounded in what we consider most important and ultimately supports us in becoming the authors of our life.

Once you have identified your core values, why not commit the rest of your life to them? Each of us is already committing our life to something that may or may not be connected to our core values. Why not commit your life to what you consider the most important? People can hold their values casually and use them on occasion, or they can treasure them and regard them as touchstones of their best intentions.

There are many ways to engage with your values on a daily basis. One powerful practice is to spend five minutes in the morning in silence, meditating on your values. Then you are ready to meet whatever the day brings with your values fresh in your mind.

Another useful practice is to write each of your core values on a sticky note and post the notes in three strategic places where you will see them during the day—for instance, at home, at work, and in your wallet or purse. Or place them where you will see one in morning, one at noon, and one at night, perhaps just before sleep.

Some people artfully print their values on high-quality paper, frame them, and hang them above their desk as personal reminders and to show their colleagues what is important to them. Others list their values as part of their yearly goal-setting, with the intention of being more accountable to them. Some organizations with ID badges have added each employee's core values to their badge to honor them. Some businesses offer to print employees' values on their business cards.

Above all, committing to core values and strengthening them through reflection and engagement allows us to respond better when we encounter injustice or other social ills that offend us. The ability to recall our core values at such pivotal times is an important first step in acting as leaders for the common good.

EXERCISES
Choosing Three Core Values

The best way to commit to personal values is to first select three as core values. Having only three core values makes it easy to recall them instantly and cultivate a working relationship with each of them so they can influence how we make choices. To choose your three core values, follow the instructions below.

Step One

Read through the following list of common values, then add to the list other values you like. The three blank lines at the bottom of the right-hand column are provided for this purpose, but they are not meant to set a limit. Feel free to add as many values as you wish.

In considering which values to add, reflect on all aspects of your life—your home environment, work space, and activities in your community. Also think about values suggested by your culture, your ancestors, your family traditions, and your own life's defining moments.

Peace	Truth
Wisdom	Integrity
Status	Love
Family	Friendship

Fame	Justice
Wealth	Influence
Power	Happiness
Authenticity	_____
Joy	_____
Success	_____

The rest of the exercise involves refining your list by choosing the values that mean the most to you. As you make your selections, consider what your intellect tells you but also listen to your heart, intuition, and spirit, each of which has its own form of wisdom. Take two to three munutes to complete each of the following steps.

Step Two

Reduce your list to ten values.

Step Three

Reduce your list to five values.

Step Four

Reduce your list to three values. These are your three core values.

○

REFLECTION QUESTIONS

* What are your three core values?

* Who are three principle-centered leaders you admire?

* In your view, how have their values provided them with stability, direction, and clarity of purpose?

* How might your personal values help you connect with the values of an organization with which you are affiliated?

5 Embracing the Wisdom of the Margins

AFRICAN AMERICAN abolitionist and humanitarian Harriet Ross Tubman was born into slavery in 1819 in Dorchester County, Maryland. Whipped repeatedly as a young child, at the age of twelve she was seriously injured by a blow to the head. Consequently assigned to house duties, she learned the workings of the household. She also explored the lay of the land surrounding the plantation. Harriet began to weave these threads of knowledge together in the hope of formulating a plan to escape from slavery.

One evening when Harriet was thirty, a white abolitionist neighbor gave her a slip of paper on which were written two names plus directions telling her how to find the first refuge on her path to freedom. There she was put into a wagon, covered with a sack, and driven to her next destination. A series of abolitionists helped her journey northward through the eastern Maryland countryside toward the Mason-Dixon Line.

In the North, she settled in Philadelphia, where she savored the taste of freedom. She knew she could never be free, however, until all slaves were free. So at the risk of capture and death, she returned to the plantation in Maryland to help others find their way to freedom.

Soon Harriet became known as one of the most courageous "conductors" of the Underground Railroad, the secret network of free blacks and white abolitionists who assisted escaped slaves on their flight north. She developed a long list of safe houses and abolitionists. She also knew the woods and coastline of Maryland like the back of her hand. Since most of the railroad travel happened at night, she taught herself how to find her way by the stars. In all, Tubman made nineteen trips back to the South and helped three hundred slaves walk to their freedom.

After the Civil War, Tubman settled in Auburn, New York, and dedicated her leadership skills to the cause of not only newly freed blacks but also women and the poor. She collaborated with Susan B. Anthony in the women's suffrage movement. With the generous assistance of her biographer, Sarah Bradford, she bought a house on seven acres of land and turned it into a home for the poor and homeless of her community. Her work to bring care and justice to the least fortunate continued even after her death in 1913. In her will, she gifted her house to the city of Auburn for continuing its care of the homeless.[1]

International activist and politician Eleanor Roosevelt was born into a prominent New York family in 1884 and grew up in an environment of immense wealth. Yet as a young child she received little affection from her parents and was socially awkward. After her mother died when she was eight, and then her father died two years later, Eleanor was sent to live with her maternal grandmother. She continued to suffer from loneliness, however, causing her shyness and self-doubt to deepen.

When Eleanor was fifteen, her grandmother sent her to the Allenwood Academy, a boarding school for girls in England. The headmistress, Marie Souvestre, had a passion for social justice and encouraged independent thinking in her students. In that environment, Eleanor began to look past her own challenges to the social problems in the world around her, overcoming much of her shyness and self-doubt, although her socially difficult childhood left her with a lifelong sensitivity to the suffering of others.

After three years at Allenwood, Eleanor returned to New York and quickly developed a reputation on the New York political scene as an advocate for social reform. She volunteered as a social worker in the slums of the Lower East Side and joined the New York Consumers League, established to expose injustices in the workplace. After seeing firsthand overcrowded factories exploiting women and children laborers, she became active in movements for women's rights and better conditions for factory workers.

When her husband, Franklin D. Roosevelt, became president of the United States, Eleanor redefined the role of First Lady, turning the office into a force for social change. In one three-month period, she traveled 45,000 miles around the nation, visiting areas suffering from social, economic, or racial injustice. She reported regularly to Franklin, and her opinions shaped many of the reforms for which history celebrates her husband.

After Franklin's death, President Truman appointed her delegate to the United Nations, where she continued her lifelong commitment to social reform but now on a global scale, becoming a champion for universal human rights. She was elected chairperson of the committee to draft the Universal Declaration of Human Rights, and when it passed unanimously at the UN on December 10, 1948, she received a standing ovation for her achievements. Both Harriet Tubman and Eleanor Roosevelt exemplify, in different ways, how embracing the wisdom of the marginalized can advance leadership for the common good.

A marker unique to leadership for the common good is its invitation to leaders to move humanity toward more justice and caring by engaging the wisdom of the margins of society, which is all too often overlooked. The margins are places of lack and thus of need. Yet as areas where injustice most often occurs, they are also sources of the most accurate information concerning how injustice manifests and the reasons it persists. Neglecting to incorporate this knowledge into many plans for the transformation of society is what causes them to fail. Consequently leaders hoping to mend the social fabric must be willing to take a close look at its tears.

The majority of human institutions and communities are marked by a long history of inequity in some form. Human institutions and communities are frequently like a large, complex group of people around a single campfire in the wilderness on a freezing night. Some people sit close to the fire, enjoying its warmth and light, but since there is not enough room by the fire for everyone others must sit beyond the reach of the fire's benefits, at the margins.

Similarly, society's resources tend to be situated close to the centers of power, usually in the hands of a few privileged people. Those at the center tend to be unaware of the magnitude of suffering of those on the margins, who hunker down to survive with their limited resources.

This unequal access to resources and power creates a fundamental us-them dynamic in the human family. The list of who is left outside the circle of comfort differs from group to group but often includes women, people of color, sexual minorities, the disabled, the elderly, and people in Third World nations. Yet the marginalized who lack power can be found anywhere, including nuclear families, places of worship, and workplaces, depending on which individuals or subgroups are the most isolated from decision making and resource allocation.

These and other marginalized pockets of society must be explored in order to work effectively for social change. A leader can also choose to plumb the depths of her personal experience of being marginalized, as Eleanor Roosevelt and Harriet Tubman did. A vision for the common good is never a grand vision crafted out of a leader's imagination. Rather it comes from firsthand experience with the suffering caused by inequity and lack of care.

For the leader in a position of privilege, like Eleanor Roosevelt, this requires personally going to difficult places of poverty and injustice to learn from them, as she did by working on New York's Lower East Side. For a leader from the margins who understands the lack of equality and injustice found there, it means gaining access to the power and resources needed to initiate change in the margins. To marshal the resources needed to catalyze change, both types of leaders for the common good must aware of the knowledge emerging from margins.

Despite the fact that people naturally shun suffering, leaders who are committed to their core values reach out, in an act of inclusiveness, to embrace the reality of the margins. As they do so, they are shaped into vessels more capable of holding the work of leadership for the common good.

THE WISDOM OF THE MARGINS

The margins provide needed resources to leaders for the common good. One such resource is new relationships, which I think of as vital company since they are essential to furthering the common good. For the leader who comes from a privileged background, these are new associations from the margins with whom he can have direct conversations that reveal the depth of their struggle and the wisdom that can aid change. For the person born on the margins, vital company means allies in the privileged class with access to power and resources within the existing system, which they are willing to share to bring needed change.

A second resource offered by the margins is what I call street smarts. This is the vivid awareness of injustices present on the margins, including their social, political, and economic causes. The pathway to awareness is different for the marginalized person and the person of privilege, but in both cases it is experienced as an awakening.

Through vital company and street smarts, leaders for the common good gain information essential for the advancement of effective social change. For example, a manufacturing plant in Wisconsin was experiencing a sharp decline in productivity between 4:00 and 6:00 pm every day. The new young manager brought in efficiency experts to do a study, but nothing changed. The owner, now even more concerned, decided to talk to the guys on the floor about the problem. They explained that between 4:00 and 6:00 pm they were working overtime. They had not brought dinner with them and were hungry, and they were worried about how to let their families know they would be home late. They suggested that if the owner put in a vending machine so they could get something to eat and a phone so they could call home, he would probably see an improvement. The owner had both changes made, and the next day productivity increased.

A third resource offered by the margins is existential freedom. This is gained not by intellectual curiosity or emotional intelligence alone but through physically traveling to the margins and allowing that experience to shift one's point of view on the world. Existential freedom is the freedom to be fully present and fully responsible for one's life, and to live life focused on a purpose greater than oneself. It's the freedom to listen to the call of conscience and one's core values and in doing so be unencumbered by cultural mores and the opinions of others that would get in the way of pursuing changes for the common good.

For leaders of privilege, existential freedom provides the awareness that although they may still be *in* the oppressive system they are no longer *of* it. They can identify with the margins and also continue to access and use the power and resources associated with privilege as they choose. For example, when Eleanor Roosevelt was First Lady she maintained her connection with those struggling on the fringes of society, which gave her information to use in recommending innovative legislation for a just society.

For leaders from the margins, existential freedom is liberating in an equally powerful though different fashion. As they wake up to the injustices around them, they see how the system is hurting them and their peers. They realize there may well be a price to pay for challenging the system and that they are already paying a price for their passivity. They are now free to choose which type of price they are willing to pay.

Existential freedom also can provide leaders from either background the clarity to adopt a transformational leadership agenda despite the views of peers and culture. Whether one's peers are those seated comfortably around the campfire or those out in the cold and darkness, some won't like the call for change. For instance, both Eleanor Roosevelt and Harriet Tubman made their peers anxious when they challenged the system. As such leaders expand their capacity for action, they naturally become involved in a broader scope of activities for social justice and inspire others to participate. The more work they do for the common good, the more they notice additional groups that have been disenfranchised and begin to address their concerns as well.

We see this expanding field of engagement dramatically in the evolution of Martin Luther King Jr. as a leader for the common good. In the mid-1960s, when he traveled to the North and experienced racism there, he shifted his focus from the black experience in the South to the black experience nationally. Then he realized that the good of the black community could not be achieved without addressing the good of everyone else, including those opposed to the goals of civil rights. Eventually he recognized a global pattern of injustice endured by people of color around the world.

Finally, his concern extended to the poor everywhere, regardless of race. He saw how the triple evils of racism, materialism, and war worked together to maintain the status quo for the disenfranchised, and thus realized that they had to be addressed together. He expressed this view most clearly in his speech "Beyond Vietnam: A Time to Break Silence," delivered in April 1967 at New York City's Riverside Church. During that speech, in which he called on America to substitute for its neocolonialist policies a more principled view of international relations, he said: "Every nation must now develop an overriding loyalty to mankind as a whole in order to preserve the best in their individual societies. This call for a world-wide fellowship that lifts neighborly concern beyond one's tribe, race, class and nation is in reality a call for an all-embracing and unconditional love for all men."[2]

By staying connected to their experiences on the margins, leaders for the common good draw moral inspiration from an ongoing personal encounter with injustices and thus maintain the perspective and moral resolve essential for successful social change. In this way, leaders continue to be fed by the vital company and street smarts inherent in the margins, both of which lead to more creative reforms on behalf of the common good. For leaders who come from the margins, this is a matter of remembering their roots. For those who come from privilege, this means staying connected with the disenfranchised after having journeyed to the margins.

PRACTICE FOR LEADERS FROM PRIVILEGE

Going to School in the Margins

For individuals who come from a social context of privilege, an important step in becoming leaders for the common good is to leave the comforts of the campfire and physically go to the margins.

Today, privileged individuals see video clips of society's margins on the evening news or photos on the covers of weekly magazines and believe they know what it's like. They may send a donation to a local or international charity. But to be a change agent for the common good, it's not enough to phone it in. It requires physically going to the margins and experiencing the difficult truths themselves.

Although when people from backgrounds of privilege physically go to the margins they cannot really know the experiences of those who live there, they at least have a chance to look into the eyes of a mother struggling to feed her children; smell the garbage dump some families call home; and feel the heat in which men toil for wages insufficient to support their families. In Eleanor Roosevelt's case, this meant traveling through New York City's streets from its upper-class neighborhoods to the Lower East Side slums. For others it might mean traveling to a developing nation and meeting with workers on a factory floor.

People from a background of privilege may have different motivations for going to the margins. Some might seek out the experience as an adventure, while others might be passionately committed to a specific social concern and consciously choose to journey to the margins to witness conditions up close. But regardless of motivation, the personal encounter with the bitter reality of life on the periphery touches their hearts and minds, intensifies their compassion, and recalibrates their vision and sense of purpose. For example, a colleague in Seattle was enjoying a career as an attorney when one day, as part of a spiritual retreat, he volunteered at a local homeless shelter. Through that firsthand encounter with the dispossessed, he was inspired to leave his profession and work on behalf of the homeless community full-time, directing one of the most effective shelters in the city.

When leaders are transformed by the margins into informed and inspired allies of the dispossessed, their leadership naturally reflects that inner shift. Such individuals may begin to question the oppressive systems they might have previously accepted as the norm. We can see such a shift reflected in the life of Oscar Romero, archbishop of the Catholic Church in El Salvador. When he became archbishop, he was known as a mild-natured, scholarly cleric and was oblivious to the brutality that the thirteen ruling families—the oligarchy of El Salvador—inflicted on the poor. Then one evening Rutilio Grande, a local priest who worked with the poor, invited him to the countryside. To his horror, Romero witnessed heavy machinery dumping dirt on a mass grave of villagers who had been massacred by the military, the brutal henchmen of the oligarchy. From that day forward, the archbishop's eyes were open to the misery of the poor and the impudence of the wealthy. Consequently, he became a champion for the poor and a force for justice in his homeland, speaking for the marginalized and challenging the ruling elite to stop their oppressive policies.

Encounters with those on the margins shape leaders by offering them an unfiltered view of the injustices in their own backyard as well as the world, and, like Oscar Romero, they may experience a liberating disillusionment, or dissonance. For instance, as leaders in the United States experience suffering and poverty in the ghettos and barrios, they more clearly comprehend how prejudiced systems create and maintain injustices, and may hear a voice inside say, "I thought America was the land of opportunity." As leaders experience such dissonance between what is and what ought to be, they are faced with a psychological dilemma: they must either deny what they now know or embrace the dissonance and work to close the gap.[3]

Hans Magnus Enzensberger's "song for those who know" reveals the subtlety of denial on the part of the privileged, the deft fashion in which they dance with what they know yet do not really want to see:

something must be done right away
that much we know
but of course it's too soon to act
but of course it's too late in the day
oh we know

we know that we're really rather well off
and that we'll go on like this
and that it's not much use anyway
oh we know . . .

and we also know that we can't help anybody really
and that nobody really can help us
oh we know . . .

and that we are extremely gifted and brilliant
and free to choose between nothing and naught
and that we must analyze this problem very carefully
and that we take two lumps of sugar in our tea
oh we know

we know all about oppression
and that we are very much against it
and that cigarettes have gone up again
oh we know

we know very well that the nation is heading for real trouble
and that our forecasts have usually been dead right
and that they are not of any use
and that all this is just talk
oh we know . . .[4]

Working to close the gap between what is and what ought to be is usually a difficult path. It means opening ourselves to pain but also to growth. Part of each of us loves comfort and security and prefers to avoid work. But, as Jungian analyst James Hollis points out, we also have a deeper part that loves adventure, purpose, and meaning.[5] This part is brought to life when we work for the common good. The most powerful choice a leader can make is to engage in a struggle with the forces that perpetuate injustice.

Even people from a background of privilege experience marginalization in some form at some point in their lives. We see this in Eleanor Roosevelt's life when she felt isolated. While people naturally prefer to distance themselves from these personal experiences, in fact they are key to empathizing with the suffering of others and developing a desire to change systems that cause that suffering.

In my case, I was the smallest kid in my junior high school and also shy, uncoordinated, and a poor student. As a result, I endured bullying, rejection, loneliness, and the fear of living in a disadvantageous position. To my surprise and delight, during the summer between my junior and senior years in high school I grew six inches, put on thirty-five pounds, and began to blossom as an athlete and student. When I went to college, I enjoyed academic success, some modest athletic prowess, and popularity among my peers, serving as a student leader. In retrospect, however, the life experiences that I consider the most instructive in orienting me to be an agent of social change were not my college days but my time feeling marginalized in junior high school when I was not invited around the campfire. However tempting it might be to subjugate such difficult memories to the past and leave them unexamined, a person's experiences of being marginalized offer important insights into the suffering of others.

When people from a background of privilege go to the periphery, they often arrive with the plan of being a "helper." This attitude, though well intentioned, is born of the unconscious assumption that individuals in need are somehow *less than* the ones offering support. This "up-down" attitude, usually expressed as charity, can produce some good but is limited. A better attitude is not to see them only in terms of their marginalized experience and to treat them generally in a more egalitarian way—as equal human beings.

This point was brought home to me one evening when a few of us from my church served dinner at a Seattle homeless shelter. On our previous visit, which had been our first, we had stayed behind the serving line and greeted the hungry homeless men with a quick hello as we dished up plates of food. On this second visit, we went beyond the safety of the kitchen to eat with these men. Awkward at first, the conversations gradually became more natural, and some of the men began to tell their stories. Later, one member of our group said, "I was shocked. I met a former Boeing engineer who lost his job, then his family and his home, and is now on the streets. Talking with him blew my stereotypes of the homeless right out of the water!"

The most fruitful stance toward the disenfranchised is a posture of humility informed by a readiness to learn, realizing that those on the margins have essential insights into the nuances of their social situation and how their peers get hurt and trapped by unjust systems and structures that surround them. Robert Terry, leadership educator and civil rights activist, flipping the term for the normal power dynamic, calls this posture "down-up."[5] In such interactions, the person of privilege sits at the feet, as it were, of the person on the margins, believing that when it comes to injustice the marginalized have the right and the credentials to be our teachers. This means setting aside assumptions about what is true and instead listening openly to their firsthand experiences on the periphery. Such an inversion of the typical power dynamic—where the marginalized person claims her power and dignity and the privileged person assumes a posture of humility and curiosity—offers both parties the chance to see and act in a new way. As people spend time together in this transforming posture, they begin to recognize how unjust systems entrap both of them and how their liberation is intertwined. As trust builds, information flows more freely, and insights into what is broken and how to fix it become more evident.

An example of inverting the typical power dynamic occurs in episodes of the television show *Undercover Boss*. For instance, the April 2010 episode chronicled Rick L. Arquilla, CEO of Roto Rooter. Leaving the comforts of the office and going incognito to join his employees in the trenches, he put his assumptions aside and became his employees' apprentice, crawling under porches, clearing sewer lines, and trying to handle the complexities of the dispatch office. Toward the end of the show, Arquilla, speaking before a gathering of Roto Rooter employees about his recent excursion into the realities of their daily lives, explained that he had gone undercover to learn more about the company and wound up having a more powerful experience of empathy than he had ever imagined. He wept as he reflected on his employees' willingness to do their difficult, often unsavory work with such concern for customers. He laughed when he recalled that he had been unable to operate the computerized dispatch system that he had helped create, and he promised to work with the employees to design a simpler system. He thanked his employees for their dedication and confessed that he had learned a great deal from them about how to make the company a better place to work.

By approaching his employees on equal ground, Arquilla acquired vital company. His close association with the workers provided him with street smarts about what Roto Rooter was doing well—offering top-notch service to customers. The workers also helped him see that the company was not giving workers the same respect they were asked to give customers. Arquilla was shaped by his experience on the margins and, as a result, was able to reshape his company in ways that benefited his employees and his customers.

PRACTICE FOR LEADERS
FROM THE MARGINS
Claiming Self-Worth

For individuals who come from the margins of society, an important step in becoming leaders for the common good is to gain awareness of their own self-worth even while living in the midst of an unjust culture. It is easy for the dominant culture to undermine the self-worth of people on the periphery and for them to buy into the idea that they are less important than others and deserving of mistreatment. When marginalized persons begin to perceive themselves as having dignity and self-worth while living in unjust situations, they often experience internal dissonance. They can't reconcile the thoughts "I am somebody" and "I am nobody" and must let go of one of them. This can be the first step toward awakening to their own potential capabilities as leaders for the common good.

During the Civil Rights Movement, when the Memphis garbage workers went on strike they weren't carrying signs that protested wages or working conditions. Their signs read: "I am a man." Dr. Martin Luther King Jr. knew that once his people had regained their human dignity, they would begin to recognize the injustices around them. Similarly, members of today's gay/lesbian communities embrace a sense of dignity and self-worth. This new perspective of themselves allows them to see the injustices in their midst with more clarity and reject homophobia as a violation of their human rights.

As people who endure social injustice gain awareness of the dissonance between what is and what ought to be, they become inspired to serve as change agents for the good of their people and the redemption of the greater society. At this point, they, like their privileged counterparts, are faced with the choice of either denying the situation or embracing it and working to change it. For marginalized individuals, denial often takes the form of internalized oppression, the third and culminating form of oppression within a threefold schema of social oppression.

First, oppression is individualized—for instance, when a single, more fortunate person may have biased views toward women or the gay/lesbian community. Second, oppression is institutionalized, as when biased sentiments become embedded in institutions, resulting in oppression such as gender-biased educational or economic inequality. Third, once an entire group has been beaten down enough by individual and institutionalized oppression, members of the group begin to practice internalized oppression. For example, a woman who has been told by countless individuals as well as educational systems that she is unequipped for the rigors of an engineering degree might internalize this biased view, thus participating in her own oppression by not filling out an application and following her dream.

People who live on the margins of society already have street smarts since they cannot afford to be oblivious to the reality of the margins. For instance, low-income parents know the flaws and loopholes of the Food Stamps or Medicaid programs because it is too costly not to know. Similarly, people living in the backcountry of Central America see how NAFTA hurts their families and how United States foreign policy has brought death and hardship to their neighbors. They do not want oppressive government policies requiring them to grow crops they cannot eat and sell them for a price that keeps them poor. They want land reform and the ability to grow their own crops so they can feed their families and earn a little extra money to send their children to school and enjoy a few modest pleasures.

A significant challenge for people on the margins is to embrace their street smarts and put these gifts to work by trying to reform the system for the common good. They accomplish this by struggling with the forces of oppression until they find a better way forward. To do so, they must ignore the voices that say, "You can't fight city hall" and listen instead to their deeper inner voices that remind them injustices need to be changed. Then, as they find their own inner strength, they will be better equipped to deal with any push back of the system. Working to change the system is not easy; but with a new sense of self-worth and some ingenuity, progress becomes possible for people on the margins.

On a trip to El Salvador, I experienced such ingenuity for progress. I met two women who had taken a leadership stance to put what they knew into action. They decided to stop growing crops for global fruit companies and to instead direct their energy to starting an egg business. They raised chickens for eggs, which they sold to other villagers for less than the normal market price and still made a profit. As a result, their family income was more consistent because it was not dependent on the volatility of global food prices, their neighbors could purchase eggs at a better price, and their successful entrepreneurism increased their confidence and self-respect.

For leaders from the margins, vital company helps them recognize their dignity and self-worth, as well as access society's power and resources. Vital company can take two forms. One form could be a peer from the margins who is farther along the path to empowerment and can serve as a mentor. Malcolm X experienced this kind of vital company. While in prison for six and a half years, he began to find new meaning for his life by becoming a voracious learner, reading in his cell until late in the evenings. His search for meaning deepened after his brother Reginald wrote to tell him about his recent conversion to Islam. Eventually, Malcolm became intrigued with the Muslim tradition and wrote to Elijah Muhammad, leader of the Nation of Islam in the United States. Through the influence of Reginald and Elijah Muhammad, Malcolm quit smoking and eating pork and began to atone for his earlier life through submission to Allah, the heart of Islamic practice. These two black men helped Malcolm broaden his perspective to see that he did not have to be a victim of the cultural bias existing in the United States and that he could create a new life as a formidable prophetic leader for justice—something no white person could have done for Malcolm at that point in his life.

The other form of vital company could be someone from a more privileged background who can act as an ally. For example, white abolitionists helped Harriet Tubman find her way to freedom and then assist others to do the same. Similarly, when nations around the world chose to divest their holdings from companies doing business in South Africa in the mid-1980s, it gave the black leadership of South Africa access to global leverage and encouragement to persist in their work for social justice. Twenty years earlier, César Chávez and the migrant farmworkers he represented gained support for their struggle for justice from those in the majority culture who joined their boycott and refused to buy grapes.

Whether leaders for the common good begin from a place of privilege in a social setting or from the margins, the question "Am I in the third circle?" invites them to open up to whatever their personal experience of the margins may be and let it transform them. For privileged leaders, the question is an invitation to turn off the internal tapes that may start to run amidst the reality of the margins, especially those that seek to blame the victim rather than wrestle with the institutionalized injustices with which the marginalized struggle.

For leaders who begin from the margins, the question "Am I in the third circle?" becomes an opportunity to break the hold of internalized oppression. They realize that if they are committed to the good of *all*, then that includes them and their group. At this moment they can turn off the tapes that say they and others in the margins are not deserving of care or justice, thus awakening to their own humanity.

For leaders of privilege and leaders from the margins, the change they envision can best be accomplished when they access the wisdom existing in the margins. Armed with the necessary knowledge of what is not working on the periphery of society and fortified by new allies, they can move forward to rectify the injustices on their watch.

EXERCISES

Taking an Inventory of Your Experiences on the Margins

If you view yourself as a person of privilege in your community, institution, or nation, consider how has that status has shaped your identity and how experiences on the margins have changed your life and leadership as you reflect on the following questions:

* How has your life been enhanced or diminished by your experience as an individual of privilege?

* How have you explored the margins in your own social settings?

* What are three steps you can take to have a more direct experience on the margins?

* What have you discovered on the margins, and how is that experience informing your life?

* Have you ever felt marginalized, and if so, how?

* How might your experience of being marginalized add value to your leadership capacity?

If you view yourself as marginalized by the culture in your community, institution, or nation, consider how that has shaped your identity, life, and leadership as you reflect on the following questions:

* How has your life been enhanced or diminished by your experience as a person of the margins?

* What unjust systems are negatively affecting your life?

* What are three steps you can take to pursue your own awakening and enhance your sense of self-worth?

* What can you do to help your peers on the margins experience their own awakening?

O

REFLECTION QUESTIONS

* How is your approach to leadership informed by the following resources of the margins?
   Vital company
   Street smarts
   Existential freedom

* If you are in a position of privilege, how could you take a refresher course on the margins?

* If you are in a marginalized position, how can you move toward liberating yourself and reclaiming your dignity and sense of self-worth? Who might be your allies?

6 Crafting a Vision

MUHAMMAD YUNUS was born in 1940 in Chittagong in eastern Bengal, India, which became East Pakistan in 1947 and Bangladesh in 1971. He completed his bachelor's and master's degrees in his homeland and a doctorate in economics at Vanderbilt University in Nashville, Tennessee, then taught economics at Middle Tennessee State University for a few years. In 1972, however, a year after Bangladesh became an independent nation-state, Yunus returned to his country eager to contribute to its future.

After accepting the position of chairman of the economics department at Chittagong University, he realized that the opportunity to apply his economic ingenuity for the good of his country lay just outside the campus in the impoverished village of Jobra. His vision was to help his country, but he knew he needed to start with a single village. As he said later, "I decided I would become a student all over again and the people of Jobra would be my professors. . . . When you hold the world in your palm and inspect it only from a bird's eye view, you tend to become arrogant—you do not realize that things get blurred when seen from an enormous distance. I opted instead for 'the worm's eye view.' I hoped that if I studied poverty at close range, I would understand it more keenly."[1]

Over the next decade, Yunus refined his vision based on various successes and failures, yet staying true to its core: to economically improve the lives of the poorest Bangladeshi people. Yunus first noticed that during the dry season the fields around Jobra lay barren, while nearby fields were green with second-season crops. When he inquired why, the villagers said they needed a tube well. Involving his students in the project, Yunus approached government agencies on the villagers' behalf and acquired a well for Jobra.

After three years, however, the fields were again barren in winter, this time because of bickering in the village over how to share the well and its costs. So Yunus helped the villagers form a cooperative among the landowners, the farmers, and himself. He would finance the project with a personal loan, and all parties would split the profits. When the villagers failed to repay Yunus after the first year, he realized they had developed a stance of learned helplessness. Knowing that local initiative fosters self-reliance, he encouraged the villagers to take responsibility for the next year's loan themselves.

Over time, the village cooperative prospered, and profits increased. However, even though the lives of many Jobra residents had improved, Yunus saw that the landless poor, most of whom were women, still suffered. He also noticed that when funds were put in the hands of the women, they tended to invest the profits in their families' health and education. Realizing that economic liberation of the women could have a cascading effect on children and other villagers, he chose to invest in them.

Because the bank did not believe poor village women would repay a loan, Yunus undersigned for the financing of US $68.00 of raw materials for forty-two women to pursue cottage industries such as weaving bamboo furniture. Yunus remained concerned about repayment, but by now he understood the psychology of village life and made the loans available to individual women who belonged to a group of five borrowers, staggering their access to the loans. If the first two members of a group were paying back their loans, after two months two more members were allowed to take out loans. If these loans were repaid, then after two more months, the fifth member received her loan. As the program matured, 99 percent of the women repaid their loans. Yunus had arrived at a winning formula.

Subsequently, his vision of funding small businesses at the village level evolved into the Grameen Bank, a community-based bank that provides loans to the poor. The bank's success, in turn, spawned the global microcredit movement, including groups such as Kiva, Lend for Peace, and the Microloan Foundation.

In 2006, the Nobel committee awarded the Nobel Peace Prize to Yunus and the Grameen Bank. The prize announcement read, in part: "Muhammad Yunus has shown himself to be a leader who has managed to translate visions into practical action for the benefit of millions of people, not only in Bangladesh, but also in many other countries."[2] Muhammad Yunus is a leader who exemplifies the crafting of a vision to bring social change.

Crafting a vision helps leaders for the common good move forward with purpose and direction. First, their core values give them an inspired sense of how the world ought to be—institutions and communities marked by love, integrity, or equity. Then embracing the margins of society with which they are concerned gives them a visceral experience of how things actually are. The discrepancy between what is and what ought to be creates tension in leaders' minds and hearts. And from the crucible of that tension, a vision of what could be—how injustices can be rectified—evolves.

A vision articulates a preferred future. The spirit of possibility inherent in a vision is expressed in the following words, adapted from George Bernard Shaw and popularized by Robert Kennedy during his 1968 presidential campaign: "Some men see things as they are and say, why; I dream things that never were and say, why not."[3]

A vision is also medium for inspiring others to roll up their sleeves and join in the work of shaping the future. Such a vision lifts people's sights above the hard work in front of them and gives purpose to their lives, as illustrated by the following story. A woman walked by three stonemasons busy laying bricks. Curious, she stopped and asked them what they were doing. One said, "I'm laying bricks." Another said, "I'm building a wall." The third mason responded, "I'm building a cathedral." The three masons were engaged in the same work, but only the third mason's work was connected to a grand vision, giving this mason purpose and the incentive to lay his bricks with greater care so his work would stand the test of time.

Finally, a vision is a picture of what *could* be, assuming that people will do the necessary work to effect such a transformation. A crystal clear vision of what could be, one that remedies the injustice witnessed in the margins, sweeps the cobwebs from a leader's mind, redirects her heart and feet, and galvanizes her commitment to engage in noble work she is called to do but has somehow forgotten. Thus, it is important that a leader for the common good adequately defines the steps that will realize the vision, setting goals and designing an action plan.

CONCEIVING A VISION

A vision for the common good is conceived in the gap between what is—a leader's experience of an injustice happening in a particular time and place—and one's moral sense of what ought to be. Direct experience with the injustices of the margins of society gives leaders knowledge of what is. A leader's moral conviction, rooted in personal core values, provides information about what ought to be, a vision of how injustices can be transformed in light of the common good. For example, leaders who have a core value of love may see a village of hungry children and develop a vision to diminish world hunger. Leaders who have a core value of family might look at the incarceration rate of inner-city youth of color in their city and have a vision of improving the lives of someone else's son or daughter. And leaders who have the core value of integrity might compare the budgets for the Departments of Defense and Education, wondering, "How does this choice prepare the next generation to become informed citizens who can safeguard the democracy?" and cultivate a vision for changing these funding ratios.

The way a vision can be catalyzed by a specific experience is further illustrated by the following story. In 1997, Ryan Hreljac was six years old and in first grade when his teacher, Mrs. Prest, presented a lesson on water and thirst. Deeply moved, he reported later: "When I learned that there were people dying in the world because they didn't have clean water, I couldn't believe it! I take nine steps, and I have it. Clean water right in my tap."[4] In response, he raised $2,000 to dig a well in Uganda. Since then, his initial vision to create one well has grown into the Ryan's Well Foundation and has brought clean water to over 700,000 people in sixteen countries.

Living with the tension between what is and what ought to be can cause a leader sleepless nights or an ache in the pit of the stomach. Escaping into denial is often a real temptation, but the more rewarding way of facing such awakening is to remain open to the generative energy associated with the tension and wait for the arrival of a vision of how to create what ought to be.

Visions may take time to develop or they may emerge quickly, and they can arrive in a variety of ways. Visions can be born with an individual's flash of insight. We have all had moments—perhaps while stepping out of the shower, before falling asleep, or during a walk in nature—when we are suddenly aware of a new, potentially powerful idea, as if we had been struck by a bolt of lightning. But visions can also arise from group discussion or action. For example, in 1965, retired millionaires Millard and Linda Fuller visited Koinonia Farm, a Christian cooperative community in Americus, Georgia. Inspired by the spirit of cooperation they observed among the farm members, the Fullers began a conversation with the founder, Clarence Jordan, about whether the principles of cooperative work could be applied to solving other social problems. Through conversations over the next several years in the context of this dedicated community, the vision for Habitat for Humanity was conceived.

Evaluating a Vision for the Common Good

Once a vision intended to advance the common good is conceived, the leader can evaluate its merit and potential effectiveness by applying to it the following four criteria rooted in the four cornerstones of leadership for the common good: whether it honors the leader's core values; whether it improves the lot of people on the margins; whether it bridges the us-them divide; and whether it articulates concern for the urgency of change.

Honoring the Leader's Core Values

If a vision honors a leader's core values, then it is likely grounded in principle and will fill the leader with the moral capacity to stay and work. We can also be confident that it will direct us toward the common good.

A vision that honors a leader's core values makes the leader feel good—excited, peaceful, or happy. This feeling relieves the tension felt between what is and what ought to be.

A vision that honors a leader's core values also fills the individual with passion and commitment to see the vision through to fruition. We do the world a favor not by tinkering with the possibility of change, as if refining our vision were a hobby we pay attention to when it is convenient, but by being fully committed to change. Muhammad Yunus didn't say, "I've got an open weekend, I think I'll go do something in Jobra." Because he had passion and commitment, every roadblock turned into a moment for learning, and every setback was a chance to choose hope. Passion became his vessel, curiosity the rudder, and hope the wind in his sails. His vision was sure to bear fruit because it was well aligned with his core values.

Improving the Lot of People on the Margins

If a vision addresses the needs and interests of people on the margins of society, and reflects a leader's courage to be a steward of the resources at the campfire for the sake of transformation, it is a vision for the common good. Such a vision employs justice and encourages the transformation of systems and structures that maintain injustice in a social setting. It can then be effective in challenging the status quo to improve the lives of those beyond the leader's own family, group, and community.

Leadership for the common good always means caring about justice for the least fortunate and most vulnerable within the broader social circles in which a group operates. For example, leaders of a nation who ignore their own habitual mistreatment of an ethnic minority within its boundaries cannot claim to be stewards of the common good just because they campaign for better health benefits for members of the president's cabinet.

Initiatives that improve the lot of those on the margins may disrupt the lives of the privileged. There is a saying in Jewish scholarship that the words of a prophet simultaneously bring comfort to the afflicted and affliction to the comfortable. A vision for the common good is likely to do the same—bring comfort to those on the margins and some anxiety to the more privileged. The work of advancing the common good is not a popularity contest. Leaders for the common good know their vision has struck a vital chord if on occasion they feel like they are being chased by the hounds of hell. If they are not, they probably haven't gone deep enough into the center of the problem.

Bridging the Us-Them Divide

A vision for the common good reminds people of their interconnectedness—that we all share the same DNA and global future—and reflects a commitment to bridge the us-them divide among those within social circles.

A vision for the common good draws wide circles that invite all into a mutually beneficial future. Unfortunately, schisms can be created even during the work of garnering support for a vision. When a vision for change begins to be implemented with finger-pointing and blame directed at defenders of the status quo, us-them strategies and more division are guaranteed. Bridging the us-them divide requires leaders to exchange blame and scapegoating behaviors for care and inclusiveness, the benefits of which are illustrated in the following true story.

A CEO of a regional healthcare system made a startling announcement to the staff, saying, in essence: "As of today there is a new policy in this hospital. If a patient is injured or dies as a result of our negligence, I intend to call the family myself and tell the truth. No one in this hospital will be in trouble alone. We will learn together. I will tell the family, 'I am deeply sorry to report that your loved one has suffered or died because of our neglect. If you intend to sue us, we will admit our wrongdoing in court just as honestly as I am sharing the truth with you now. I also give you my pledge that we will continue to study what happened so that we will learn from this tragedy, for the sake of our institutional integrity and so that your loved one will not have died in vain.'" Since his announcement, patient safety has increased dramatically, and although he has had to make several actual calls due to injury and death, to date the healthcare system has not been sued. He reached out and led for the good of the patients, their families, and his employees. In his vision, everyone had worth and deserved justice and care.

A vision for the common good helps people reconnect with one another, the planet, and their own core goodness. For instance, Abraham Lincoln's vision reconnected South and North; Rachel Carson's vision connected humans with the environment; and Yunus's vision reconnected the poor with their own dignity.

Articulating Concern for the Urgency of Change

If a vision is filled with a moral imperative that articulates concern for the urgency of change, it is a vision for the common good. When poverty, hunger, homelessness, or oppression in any form has a face and a name, we naturally want to respond in a timely way. Eleanor Roosevelt reportedly worked eighteen-hour days to craft and win support for the Universal Declaration for Human Rights, driven by a deep sense of exigency, informed by her face-to-face encounters with human need.

Similarly, in December of 1954 Harry and Bertha Holt saw a film depicting the desperate needs of Amerasian children living in South Korean orphanages. Immediately the Holts sent money and clothes, but they felt prompted to do more—they wanted to give these children a family. They decided to adopt eight children but soon learned that it was impossible unless they could get both houses of Congress to pass a special law allowing for international adoption. The couple promptly began work on this daunting challenge. Harry left for Korea to be with the children, while Bertha lobbied Congress. Just nine months after the Holts saw the film of the Amerasian children, the Holt Bill passed Congress, paving the way for international adoption in general and enabling Harry to bring home their eight children that same month.

Five months later, Harry traveled back to South Korea to begin helping American families give other children a home, and in 1956 the Holt Adoption Agency was incorporated. To date the agency has helped forty thousand children from eleven different countries connect with adoptive families.

TRANSLATING A VISION INTO ACTION

Once a vision is conceived, the leader implements it, translating it into action, which calls on the leader's capacity for strategic planning. Several strategies can help the leader implement the vision: sharing the vision first with a few trusted allies; paying attention to the history and politics of the community or institution the vision will affect; fine-tuning the vision based on feedback; and anticipating resistance to the vision's goals and aspirations.

Sharing the Vision with Trusted Allies

Although the vision will eventually be shared with the broader community, early on it is best to share it with only a few trusted allies who will listen to the leader's dream with interest and openness. A new vision is delicate cargo and should be handled with care.

Exposing the new idea to general critique is to risk letting it be dismissed as an impractical dream. Even after revealing it to allies such as friends and coworkers, leaders must maintain a balance between adhering to the essence of the original vision and remaining open to useful feedback that will help them fine-tune the vision.

Sometimes trusted allies can offer the practical advice needed to implement the vision. During a weeklong retreat focused on a Buddhist view of leadership, I heard a surprising comment on this point by Omori Sogen Rotaishi, founder of the Chozen-ji Zen Dojo in Honolulu. He said the leader is the visionary, inspired by love dedicated to making the world a better place. The love-inspired leader often needs to be supported by a tactical strategist who cares for the leader and the vision and knows how to get things done.[5] This partnership frees the leader to dream big dreams, knowing that a trusted ally is willing to carefully tether them to the practicalities.

The Zen master's point reminded me of Don Quixote, a romantic dreamer who loses touch with reality in the novel with the same name by Miguel de Cervantes. A lesser known but essential character is Sancho Panza, Quixote's pragmatic man-servant and faithful follower who believes in the dreamer but is also more connected to reality. Without Panza, Quixote strays into madness, yet Quixote gives Sancho a chance to pursue the impossible dream. A dreamer like Don Quixote can give his followers wings, while followers like Panza give the leader landing gear.

Both visionary and pragmatist elements are necessary in translating a vision into action. Often an individual has both capacities, such as Muhammed Yunus. A leader who tends too much toward idealism, however, is wise to find a Sancho, whose pragmatic attention to the real details can manifest the vision.

Paying Attention to Politics and History

As a leader translates a vision into action, it is necessary to pay attention to the history and politics of the particular region, institution, or element of society that will be affected, especially if the leader is new to the place. I discovered this early in my career in higher education, at a time when I thought vision and passion were enough to effect change. During one of our weekly meetings, my supervisor gave me some important feedback. Knowing I liked baseball, he said, "Bill, I am happy to report that you have the best fastball on the team, but unfortunately it is your only pitch." We laughed, then he coached me to see that making change happen meant I needed to get to know the people, traditions, and the formal and informal power brokers on campus and in the surrounding community.

To study the political moorings of the locale, the leader could ask such questions as: How does change happen around here? Who are the power brokers who can get in the way or open doors, depending on how and when they hear about the vision? Who needs to be at the table because the vision touches their institution, people, or territory?

In addition, the leader should research the local history, considering such questions as: Has anything like this vision been tried before? Did it fail or succeed, and why? What can I learn from these earlier initiatives?

By doing this homework, the leader can learn from the past and develop more potential allies to help implement the vision. When we take the time to connect with people who know the territory, invariably they are grateful to be asked. Often, as a result of hearing our vision, they offer to use their social capital by making an introduction or giving an endorsement, thus paving the way for implementation of the vision.

Fine-Tuning the Vision

As a vision is translated into action, the leader has an opportunity to fine-tune it based on interaction with allies or adversaries, as well as lessons learned in the field. Faced with any unintended consequences of implementing the vision, the leader can use such feedback to further clarify the vision.

To fine-tune a vision, the leader needs to remain committed to it while simultaneously being open to feedback from allies and adversaries alike, trusting that critique, whether well intended or ill willed can strengthen the vision. Facing difficult feedback, however ugly or inconvenient, can ultimately help increase the vision's chances of success.

For example, Muhammad Yunus continually adapted his original vision to the challenges and opportunities of the day without losing its moral essence. As each strategic plan succeeded or registered as a failure—the villagers' failure to use the tube well, their failure to pay him back, the discovery that more than five borrowers in a microloan group was too many—he took it not as a sign to quit but as feedback for modifying the vision and the plan for implementing it. His vision of economic well-being for Bangladeshi villagers remained the same, but its expression shifted according to the situation on the ground.

Anticipating Resistance

By anticipating resistance from those with other points of view, the leader can be prepared to engage wise adversaries without compromising the essence of his vision. In fact, opposition to a vision, if openly considered, may actually strengthen the vision. The goal for the leader at this point is to welcome the resistance in the spirit of third-circle inclusiveness, make an effort to understand opponents' concerns, and consider whether it is possible to address them within the vision's parameters. If the answer is yes, the vision becomes stronger and the leader gains more allies. If the answer is no, although the resistance may continue the leader can be satisfied that such opponents have been included in the process.

Not all encounters with resistance have storybook endings, but leaders can civilize situations by anticipating and welcoming the resistance in the spirit of respect and tolerance for alternative perspectives, as illustrated by the following anecdote. Marshall Rosenberg, founder of the Center for Nonviolent Communication, was in Israel conducting training for a mixed group of Israelis and Palestinians. Before the training began, someone in the crowd shouted, "You're an American. How could you possibly help Palestinians, given all that your country has done to oppose us!" Rosenberg listened intently to this person and responded with questions to better understand his concerns. After the training, the man invited Rosenberg to his home for the evening to help celebrate Ramadan with his family.

If resistance persists, not only the vision but also the visionary may be critiqued or even ridiculed. When resistance becomes personal, the leader might be dismissed as naive, idealistic, or just plain meddlesome. Leaders who experience such criticism need to engage in some form of self-support while remaining in the third circle. For example, they can recall their core values, the injustice experienced in the margins, and the moral urgency they feel because they know conditions could be better for the disenfranchised. Leaders will regain strength, focus, and commitment by returning to these moral centers.

FROM VISION TO SOCIAL INVENTION

A social invention expands a vision's potential impact beyond its original context of time, place, and leverage. Daniel H. Burnham, architect and creator of the famous Chicago Plan of 1909, once counseled city leaders: "Make no little plans, for they have no magic to stir men's blood. . . . Make big plans. Aim high in hope and work."[6] A vision for the common good yields a plan to bring change to a particular corner of the world—whether it is the sales department at a corporation, an after-school program in an inner-city school, or a cottage industry of a village in a developing nation. Yet sometimes the same vision can also bring positive change to other corners of the world. For example, although Yunus first implemented his vision to help all people of Bangladesh, by focusing on a single village he fine-tuned it until it became a replicable innovation that could be applied to benefit the poor around the world. Thus his vision evolved into a social invention.

Social inventions resulting from grand visions are often change agendas that address fundamental issues. They may take the form of public policy, such as America's Civil Rights Act of 1964, or they may spring to life in the form of an institution, like the Environmental Protection Agency and the National Park Service, which have shaped our relationship with the natural world. In addition, social inventions may take the form of ideas. That all people "are endowed by their Creator with certain unalienable Rights" is a social invention in the form of an idea, crafted by Thomas Jefferson, that continues to instigate social transformation around the world.

Social invention can expand the originally intended reach of the vision. For example, even though the women's suffrage movement initiated by Elizabeth Cady Stanton and Lucretia Mott in 1850 began as a way to gain access to social power in the form of the right to vote, it evolved into a means of improving women's rights in general. Similarly, Mothers Against Drunk Driving (MADD), the organization Candy Lightner founded after her daughter was killed by a repeat drunk-driving offender in May 1980, started with a focus on driving laws in California but grew quickly into a national social invention. The issue struck a chord across American society, and two years after the founding of MADD, President Ronald Reagan established a presidential commission on drunk driving and Congress passed a bill to support states in curbing drunk driving.

Today, with the Internet, it is easier than ever for a vision to grow quickly and for a few people to have a vast impact. Matt Flannery and Jessica Jackley founded Kiva in October of 2005, expanding upon microlending as popularized by the Grameen Bank by allowing individual " micro-funders" to interact directly with low-income "micro-entrepreneurs" in developing nations around the globe. In a matter of hours, all the loan requests they posted were funded. One year later, the PBS program *Frontline* aired a documentary on Kiva, after which the public's response overwhelmed Kiva's Web site. The following week, over $250,000 was loaned. In November 2009, a little over four years from its inception, Kiva reached $100 hundred million in total loans.[7] As this example demonstrates, a vision can morph into a social invention when the leader remains attentive to the vision's potential, allowing it to mature.

Because of their scale, social inventions foster wide-reaching and long-lasting changes for the common good. For one thing, they can make a daunting task doable, like suddenly being able to paint a barn with a power painter after having used an artist's brush. Since they hasten progress, social inventions support the idea of "the fierce urgency of now." If a vision matures into a social invention, it can result in a giant step forward for the common good.

Whenever progress is made on one vision for the common good, it sets in motion social momentum that can aid progress on others. In the 1950s, the Civil Rights Movement created social momentum that supported visions for progress in the environmental, women's rights, and disabilities movements. We personally contribute to the momentum when, as everyday people, we are grounded in our core values and able to identify social concerns to which we are passionately committed.

Any vision for the common good serves as a fractal—a reduced copy of the whole. People involved in the implementation of the vision not only help out on this particular issue but experience a foretaste of the day when the shift to a common good worldview is complete.

EXERCISES

While crafting your vision, consider your experience of the tension between what is and what ought to be and encourage your vision of what could be to emerge by following the directions below.

Making a Mural to Craft a Vision

★ Take a large sheet of paper and draw a vertical line down the middle.

★ On the left side of the line, draw a scene depicting a social concern. For example, if the social concern is homelessness, you might draw a community with people sleeping under bridges, standing in bread lines, and on corners with signs saying, "I'll work for food."

* Recall your three core values and think of a symbol for each one. For example, love could be symbolized as a heart.

* On the right side of the line, using these symbols draw a picture that transforms your social concern, what is, into an image of what ought to be. For example, you might draw homeless people walking toward a heart-shaped building where they can find help.

* Spend two to five minutes reflecting on the contrast between the two scenes.

* Write down your thoughts about how conditions could be transformed for the common good.

○

REFLECTION QUESTIONS

* What social concern causes you anguish?

* When you experience tension between the world as it is and the world as it ought to be according to your core values, what vision emerges?

* How is your vision in keeping with the common good world-view?

* How will you articulate your vision so that it resonates with the hearts, minds, and dreams of others?

* Who will be your allies in support of your vision?

* What practical considerations would you focus on in implementing the vision, based on the particular politics and history of the region, institution, or group involved?

* How will you retain the spirit of the vision as you begin to share it with possible critics?

* Does your vision have the potential to become a social invention?

7 Creating Gracious Space

FRED ROGERS, an innovator in children's television, was among the first people to recognize television as a potentially powerful medium for education. He explained, "I went into television because I hated it so, and I thought there was some way of using this fabulous instrument to be of nurture to those who would watch and listen."[1] His vision was to create a television environment for children that would support their development as future community members as well as allow them to regard themselves as inherently good and deserving of love just by being who they were. Subsequently, he designed the show *Mister Rogers' Neighborhood*, which was first broadcast on public television in his hometown of Pittsburgh in 1965, aired 895 episodes over 32 years, and won 4 Emmy Awards.

Aware from studying child development that children find comfort in a familiar, predictable environment, Rogers opened every episode with the same song and scene: coming in the door and putting on his homey cardigan sweater and tennis shoes, as he sang the words of the opening song, "Please won't you be my neighbor?"

He modeled the natural curiosity of children, asking questions of guests on the program from a child's perspective, thus honoring and validating the way children see the world and learn. The book *The World According to Mister Rogers*, a collection of Rogers' writings published posthumously in 2003, sheds light on the principles Rogers not only taught on the show but lived by: be yourself, engage the world with understanding love, and remember that we are all neighbors. Among these, perhaps Rogers' greatest influence was his consistent willingness to be his authentic self. Whether talking to his television audience, one-on-one with a child, appearing on the *Johnny Carson Show*, testifying before Congress, or mowing his lawn in his own Pittsburgh neighborhood, he was always his same soft-spoken, gentle person. Because he was able to connect intimately with his viewers, due to the program's supportive environment, he could present complex and controversial issues, such as divorce, war, and racial conflict, with an honesty that other television programs avoided. Fred Rogers is a leader who exemplifies the creation of gracious space in an environment supporting the common good of children. The principles he embodied and taught apply also to creating gracious space for adults.

Gracious space is a safe and constructive setting in which people can do the difficult transformative work necessary to advance the common good. When people hear the word *gracious*, they usually think of kindness, courtesy, and skillfulness at interaction. Yet gracious space is not just a feel-good place where people are asked to lose their edge and be polite; rather, it is a place where everyone is invited to fully engage in the work of social change for the common good. As leaders share their visions with the world—meeting with trusted confidants and colleagues, as well as diverse people who might resist them—the nature of the environment in which these interactions take place becomes important. An environment is the sum of all of the conscious and unconscious choices that inform the social, emotional, intellectual, spiritual, and moral climate of a community or organization. The nature of an environment can either limit or liberate the potential of any group, vision, or interaction between proponents and critics of a vision for the common good.

Consequently, one of the most powerful things a leader for the common good can do is to ask, "Is the existing environment the one we need to make progress toward the common good?" Such an environment, one that welcomes all and actively advances justice and care for all, can be seen as a gracious space.

Gracious space is a practical training ground for advancement of the common good. It also offers participants a foretaste of the common good as a global reality. For people within a gracious space, the common good worldview becomes a tangible experience. They begin to regard the group like a family, and the group is naturally inclined to "share the rock" out of a sense of affiliation.

Since gracious space supports the common good worldview, in gracious space the common good ethic takes precedence over the us-them ethic. The group is thus challenged to improve its group dynamics, including the ability to deal with conflict *within* the group. The idea that conflict holds potential for transformation sounds counterintuitive if not radical to most people, yet this is only because the concept is outside the realm of the culture's dominant us-them thinking. Most of us are unschooled in dealing with conflict in ways that prompt healthy discussions and fruitful results. Instead, people try to suppress differences by maintaining a surface politeness, or they default into old us-them behaviors that promote dissent and impasse. But when conflict is handled well, it becomes a doorway to desirable and creative insights for change.

In fact, conflict is a normal, even healthy outgrowth of bringing diverse points of view together. One of the fundamental assumptions concerning healthy conflict in a group is that no single person, not even the leader, can understand the issue under consideration in its entirety; rather, each person's point of view has value and must be considered.

This perspective is illustrated by a tradition among the Sioux. When they come together to discuss an important matter, an elder places a Y-shaped tree branch in a clay pot so that it is standing vertically at the center of the meeting room. Chairs are arranged in a circle surrounding the branch. The elder divides the people into four groups, inviting each to enter the circle from one of the four cardinal directions and be seated; the elder then instructs a representative from each group to describe in detail what he sees. It is noted that each person sees the branch from only one point of view and, to understand the whole, must depend on others.

Another fundamental principle of healthy conflict concerns each person's responsibility to check his intention before speaking. When a speaker is about to bring up a contentious point or pose a hard question, if his intention is to do harm it is as if he is reaching into his pocket and grabbing a rock to throw at someone else's idea. With a shift of intention, however, the same point can be offered as a gift. The key is to remember to ask: Am I bringing a rock or bringing a gift? If you're about to toss a rock, it is wise to put that thought back into your pocket and wait until you can offer a gift instead.

Gracious space is intended not as something a group engages in only once but as an environment in which the group works. As time progresses, a group's capacity to maintain gracious space will be tested. Inevitably, someone in the group will disappoint someone else, or manipulate the group's trust for their personal interest, or talk behind someone's back. This is not because the group includes some bad apples; it is simply the reality of most human communities. The question is: When such things happen, how will the group members then treat each other? If the group has the capacity to re-create gracious space after disappointing or hurting each other, then their practice of gracious space will have born fruit and they will be able to regard themselves as a learning community committed to the common good.

THE LEADER'S ROLE IN GRACIOUS SPACE

The practice of gracious space, like the practice of embracing the wisdom of the margins, asks the leader to pay attention to the territory in which people meet. In the margins, the focus is on establishing connection with those who have historically been excluded from mainstream society so that their wisdom can be brought to bear on the solutions set forth to advance a more just society. In gracious space, the focus is on how to help people with diverse perspectives interact in such a way that they advance the common good.

The leader fosters the development of gracious space in a group by first cultivating this spirit in his own life. As the qualities of gracious space inform his presence, words, and actions, he begins to embody it. Then, when he comes into a gathering of people, he models gracious space for them and invites the group to cocreate it for one another.

Creating Gracious Space with Oneself

Gracious space begins in the heart of the leader as a spirit that welcomes all, recognizes the worth of all, and engages creatively with all to cocreate a future for the good of all. Leaders cultivate this spirit by offering gracious space to themselves. This means acknowledging and accepting all parts of themselves just the way they are—with their aptitudes and their inadequacies. By accepting both our gifts and our flaws, and coming to peace with our imperfect selves, we can welcome the same in others. Practicing inclusiveness with ourselves constitutes the inner work of leadership development. It allows leaders to bring their unpretentious, authentic selves to the work of leadership for the common good.

For example, at the beginning of each day Fred Rogers created for himself the environment he would later create for others on television. He began the day with two hours of prayer and reading before sunrise. Then he went for a morning swim and had breakfast. By 8:30 am, he was ready to give to the world the same care and respect he had given to himself.

Rogers embodied gracious space so effectively that its spirit pervaded all his interactions, whether with groups or one-on-one. In his book *I'm Proud of You: My Friendship with Fred Rogers*, Tim Madigan recounts dozens of examples of gracious space made manifest through Rogers' presence, choices, and actions. Madigan reports that Rogers had an attitude of inclusiveness, reflected in his interest in everyone. During the very difficult days when Tim's brother, Steve, was dying of cancer, Rogers not only consoled Tim but reached out directly to Steve as well. Although Rogers had never met Steve, he phoned the family home and listened deeply for thirty minutes while Steve talked about how he had come to peace with his impending death.

To become effective leaders for the common good, we need to give ourselves a good measure of gracious space every day, by doing such things as calling a friend who cares for us unconditionally, going for a walk in nature, meditating, or finding other ways to connect with Spirit. When we are experiencing stress in our lives, it becomes even more important to create gracious space for maintaining the balance necessary to act as effective leaders.

Embodying Gracious Space in the Group

Having benefited from creating gracious space for themselves, leaders begin to embody its spirit. Embodying gracious space happens over time, yet each time leaders receive this gift they become more like the gift.

The spirit of gracious space that a leader embodies can permeate a group of people the way candlelight subtly illuminates a room. When gracious space is evident in the leader's presence, people sense it as an invitation to awaken the same spirit in their own hearts. As members of a group awaken this spirit, it influences how they interact with one another, shaping the group's environment. The following stories illustrate how a leader for the common good can influence a group by modeling the spirit of gracious space.

Dorothy Day, founder of the Catholic Worker Movement, a group dedicated to bringing dignity, care, and justice to the poor, was in her office meeting with a homeless woman when her secretary came to the door and said, "Excuse me, but you have an important phone call." Dorothy responded immediately, asking, "Which one of us is it for?" She did not feign respect for the homeless and poor but really saw them as fellow human beings. By embodying the spirit of gracious space with the poor, she helped launch the Catholic Worker Movement, known for its respectful engagement with the poor.

Walter Cronkite, a well-known broadcast journalist and anchorman, was in the CBS newsroom on November 22, 1963, when news arrived that President Kennedy had been shot. Immediately he took on the role of breaking the tragic news to the nation, all the while, embodying gracious space. Although his was already a trusted voice, his stature grew even more as he held the space for collective grief. His surprise when first announcing that the president had been shot, his grief as he confirmed Kennedy's death, and the calm reassurance in his voice as he narrated events of the next few days showed the nation a way forward.

Gracious space held internally allows a leader to remain centered even during high-stakes, high-pressure events. Anchored in the spirit of gracious space, the leader can then make that same gracious spirit available to others.

Inviting the Group to Cocreate Gracious Space

When inviting a group to cocreate gracious space, the leader models practices that support it. She also calls the group's attention to a vision that advances the common good or other work before the group and encourages them to create the environment needed to accomplish it. Once a group sees the work at hand, they generally want to start right in. The leader then draws their attention to the matter of the environment with a question such as: What sort of space is needed for this work, and how can we cocreate it?

The leader cannot give a group gracious space. She can only inspire, embody, and invite it through her presence and the quality of her interactions, seeding the group with the spirit of an environment marked by honesty, intent, listening, and respectful responses to conflict. Ultimately, the group members must choose to join in its cocreation.

This is illustrated by the actions of Jeff, a clinical psychologist who is gifted at working with recalcitrant youth. He was conducting a weekend workshop for a group of thirty such students in the Seattle School District. As the retreat began, the students were engaged in their own raucous interactions, ignoring him and refusing to cooperate. Jeff then brought out a bag of cookies and put it on the table next to him. The teenagers began to notice the cookies, and someone shouted, "Give them to me. I'll eat them!" Eventually, the group began to quiet down to hear what Jeff's soft voice, under the ruckus, was saying: "Any ideas on how to distribute these? Any method is fine with me as long as everyone gets the same number of cookies."

The group started brainstorming and finally came up with a plan that worked. As the young people ate their cookies, Jeff asked them another question: "How do you want me to lead the rest of the retreat? If you'd like me to be a policeman, you can act one way. If you'd like me to be a parent, you can act another. If you'd like me to be a friend, I'll adjust to that."

Jeff's actions, which initiated the cocreation of gracious space, resulted in a change of attitude and behavior among the group. Jeff had let the students know that he saw them as powerful and had invited them to link their intentions with his. With the simple exercise of determining how to distribute the cookies, the students discovered that they could influence the group's future through their choices.

PRACTICES FOR CREATING GRACIOUS SPACE

Because gracious space is a foretaste of a common good world-view, the practices that create gracious space in a group are also the practices humanity needs to develop to shape a society based on the common good. Since they challenge the us–them assumptions that undergird our usual interactions with each other, the following practices involve taking some risk, which makes us feel vulnerable. Yet working with them can have significant practical benefit in the present while giving us an opportunity to participate in the shift to a new worldview.

Welcoming the Stranger

Gracious space is designed to facilitate one of the truths about the common good—that the wisdom needed to face the challenges of the day is scattered in bits and pieces among group or community members. If that wisdom is to be secured, the group or community must be open to all contributions, even the odd, annoying, or surprising ones. Consequently, creating gracious space means welcoming the stranger into the conversation. A stranger need not be only a person we do not know; a stranger can also be a person we know whose point of view is unfamiliar or whose style or presence we find uncomfortable or annoying.

I learned what it means to welcome a stranger from the residents of a small town in Italy. My wife, Sandy, and I, in celebration of our twenty-fifth wedding anniversary, took a trip to Europe. Among our favorite spots was Vernazza, one of the five villages comprising the Cinque Terra along Italy's west coast. Our first evening in Vernazza there was a power outage, which ended up lasting two days, affecting all of France and most of Italy.

Being modern ATM-dependent travelers, most of the tourists in Vernazza had little cash on hand, and without power the ATMs were useless. Sandy and I wondered how this situation would be managed. Soon word was on the streets that if we wanted to buy a meal or make a purchase we just had to sign our names with a waiter or salesperson, and we would all settle our bills when the ATM machines came back on. Sandy and I shifted from feeling like foreigners to feeling like trusted neighbors literally overnight. Merchants and restaurant owners smiled knowingly as we entered their establishments, a reminder that the only way to deal with the situation was to get closer. This experience gave me a visceral sense of how quickly individuals can make the transition from stranger to fellow community member.

Yet people are also inclined to keep others in the position of strangers. When we estrange someone, it is as if we put out our arms like traffic policemen and say, "Stop! You're not welcome here." We put up such nonverbal stop signs for individuals in our neighborhoods, colleagues at work, and people we encounter in public places. We often do this so politely that the other person doesn't realize we have shut a door. This is one reason constructive conversations with diverse people on complex issues are rare. As soon as someone voices a conflicting point of view, we stop listening.

To cultivate gracious space, we need to recognize who we are distancing and why. For instance, a person might be surprised to discover that he puts up nonverbal stop signs more often with particular types of people—with the politically progressive, or recent immigrants, or conservative-looking businessmen, or people who are overweight. Once we see the pattern, we can choose other behaviors.

For me, the subtle sensation of putting up a stop sign has become a friendly reminder to ask myself: What is it about this person—her beliefs, her presence, her energy—that makes me want to distance myself from her? Once I become aware of the reasons for my behavior, I can consciously put aside that defense mechanism and welcome the person into my sphere.

Welcoming the stranger is not only a decent thing to do but also a smart thing to do. Someone who thinks differently may be the one to offer the very insight an individual or group needs to accomplish a goal. In her book *Team of Rivals*, Doris Kearns Goodman reveals how Abraham Lincoln knew that to find a path forward for a nation requiring healing and unity, he needed to gather a "team of rivals" as his cabinet. He wanted to be exposed to a broad spectrum of opinions expressed for a common purpose: to preserve an eighty-seven-year-old experiment in democracy.

The role of the leader is to model the welcoming of diverse people and perspectives. He does this not only with his words but also through his behavior. It is one thing to say the stranger is welcome, but it is another to openly and patiently engage people who are asking difficult questions about our vision or challenging our point of view. Us-them instincts surface, making it easy to move into a defensive or aggressive posture to protect our interests. Even so, every effort the leader makes to include a stranger encourages others to develop the same habit.

Showing Curiosity

Another practice for cultivating gracious space is curiosity. When people are developing an idea or a project in a group, they can easily fall into a competitive posture. They listen not so much to gain information but for ammunition with which to shoot down the ideas of others. Or they listen only partially because they are already forming their response to the point they think the speaker is going to make. In such an environment, conversations devolve to a series of assertions about what people already believe.

One of the best ways to get beyond ineffective us-them, point-counterpoint exchanges is to practice curiosity. In my seminars, when it's time to talk about curiosity, before I say a word I walk around the room shaking a brown paper bag. The rattling sound heard as I shake the bag lets people know there is something inside it. A few guess out loud what's in the bag. Eventually somebody asks me to show them what's inside. When I turn the bag upside down and out rolls a marking pen and maybe a roll of masking tape, people are amused and perplexed.

Then I say: "Do you know why I did that? It had nothing to do with what was in the bag. It had everything to do with you. You became so much more present, awake, and curious—and I was only holding up a bag. What keeps us from being this curious when someone in the group is holding up an idea, a point of view, or a dream?"

If people listened with wide-open curiosity, we might find ourselves exploring aspects of a question or vision we would otherwise dismiss. We might hear more people saying, "That's an interesting idea. Tell me more, especially why it is important to you." We would listen more keenly for the thread of thought, or that half-formed idea in somebody's mind, that just might be the key to a better future.

Curiosity can be surprisingly disarming in group dynamics, even when people say something outrageous or frustrating. For example, one my favorite supervisors was curious by nature and very centered. I can recall a variety of occasions when a member of our team expressed frustration or opposition during a meeting, and he would often respond with a simple comment such as: "Wow, you've got a lot of energy around this issue. Can you tell me what you're concerned about?" Often this was sufficient to turn the conversation in a fruitful direction. The person expressing frustration or opposition was provided gracious space to vent and then get back in touch with her own principled perspective. If curiosity can prompt so dramatic a shift in conversation, imagine how much good it could do at a volatile community meeting or the negotiating table of an international organization.

When group members, in both casual and intense moments, observe the leader practicing curiosity, they become more likely to show curiosity in interactions with one another. The environment of the group then shifts to one of gracious space. As the level of curiosity in the group increases, people take more risks with one another, knowing that their ideas and visions, once expressed, will be met with curiosity in gracious space. In this way, difficult questions can be better explored and resolved, paving a path toward the common good.

Building Trust

Another practice for cultivating gracious space is building trust, a basic aspect of community everywhere. Trust allows us to create and depend on the covenants, or public promises, that are essential for community to flourish. When trust is present, all parties can assume that the others have their best interest at heart. Without trust, all they have is fear.

Trust within a group is built through action—in particular, actions that require risk-taking. When I think of venturing into trust, I reflect on Baylor, a boy four years old at the time his family attended my church. One Sunday during the after-service gathering in the fellowship hall, Baylor decided he wanted to fly, and he asked me to help. He climbed up onto a long folding table and crept to the edge, looking at me with anxious eyes and an eager grin. I extended my arms toward him, and he jumped, trusting that I would catch him. That was so much fun, he decided to take a bigger risk. He climbed onto the table again, but this time he started at the far end, running the table's full length and then soaring into the air and into my waiting arms. He had taken a risk, and his trust had grown.

In a group, someone, usually the leader, must be willing to take the first, often strategic, risk to move the group toward increased trust—choosing to be vulnerable and seeing how the group responds. If others in the group recognize and honor the risk-taking and respond in kind, then trust is likely to grow. This dynamic is illustrated by the following anecdote.

Dale Nienow, a former coworker of mine, was participating in a multicultural and intergenerational gathering celebrating the importance of grassroots leadership. The facilitator asked group members to introduce themselves by sharing their name and something that was weighing heavily on their minds or hearts. The first participants mentioned things that were fairly safe and superficial. But Dale made a decision to take a risk by revealing something more personal and profound—the fact that the previous week his wife had been diagnosed with breast cancer. As introductions continued around the table, others followed his lead. Even though he was not the facilitator, his actions served as a display of leadership, resulting in a new openness and level of trust in the group.

Such risk-taking can create a foundation for building trust within a group. Once trust becomes part of the environment, the group feels capable of taking on the tough yet essential issues usually ignored. Topics such as economic, racial, and social justice or environmental stewardship can be raised because trust opens the doors to more candid conversations.

Learning in Public

Another practice for cultivating gracious space is learning in public. When people in a group feel safe enough to learn from one another—to have an ah-hah moment and let their minds be changed in front of their peers—gracious space is created and the group can progress toward its goals.

We might presume that learning in public happens all the time since adults go to school, attend seminars, and participate in community meetings. On the contrary, the norm is resistance to learning in public, caused by people's insecurities about how others might perceive them. My friend Bill Koenig, who teaches organization change and development, is fond of saying, "You can look good or you can learn in public. You just can't do both at the same time."

The classic example of learning in public is children in a park who feel free to express natural curiosity about their surroundings. They run everywhere, picking up leaves, stones, perhaps stray bits of paper to look at, smell, and maybe even taste. They are learning machines. Not knowing is unimportant to them, and they are unconcerned about looking good in the presence of others.

But while growing up, people get the message that as an adult it's not okay to not look good and therefore it's not okay not to know. This kills creative conversation and problem solving. Someone might share a wonderful breakthrough idea, but rather than group members saying, "Wow, that's a great concept. I have never heard that before. Tell us more," people nod their heads as if they already were familiar with the idea. Then the idea dies quietly, and the status quo remains firmly entrenched.

Learning in public requires people to care less about how they look and more about discovering what might really work. That inquisitive child's mind is still alive in all of us; we just need to get the self-consciousness of the adult's mind out of the way. When people are open to what is new, they are more likely to question assumptions. For example, during a school board meeting, a district superintendent, hoping to inspire a discussion about dramatically reforming the school year calendar, might decide to question what everyone takes for granted, asking, "What was the original rationale for starting the school year in September?" Once the group is reminded that the existing model for public education was developed in an agricultural society, when the students were needed on the farms during summer, they are freer to think outside the box. The leader might then propose a more challenging follow-up question: "How would our models for schools be transformed if we replaced the agrarian model with a model for a global information society?"

Leadership in this complex global century is not about having the final, definitive answer; it is about having transformative questions that could advance the common good and not being afraid to ask them at the right time and in the right setting. One of the most powerful things a leader can do to promote learning in public is to set aside the demeanor of being the expert and have the courage to say, "I don't know." This gives everyone permission to let out their inquisitive three-year-old. When not knowing is okay, people are more likely to replace point-counterpoint debate with creative dialogue. A debate assumes that one side knows the truth and must persuade the other side to join their way of thinking. Dialogue assumes the truth is yet to be discovered and that it is found through listening to all viewpoints.

Being Your Authentic Self

Perhaps the simplest practice that fosters gracious space is to be our authentic selves. Authenticity is the net result of discovering who we truly are and having the courage to be just that. As simple as this may sound, it is also enormously challenging; yet once individuals cultivate this way of being, it sends out a vibration of unpretentious ease that registers with others. By contrast, individuals are inauthentic if the way they present themselves is at odds with their core identity. If people pretend to be something they are not or speak with insincerity, their inauthenticity is usually sensed by observers or listeners.

People are naturally attracted to authenticity and turned off by inauthenticity. When we opt to be our authentic selves, we are choosing to be human, a word that shares the same root as the word *humility*. It is important to realize that humility is not self-deprecation but the natural result of no longer pretending that perfection is an option. Peace comes from eliminating pretense and simply being ourselves.

When leaders dare to be their authentic selves, they claim personal power. Fred Rogers demonstrated the power of authenticity in the context of leadership not only on his television show but in all contexts, including during his testimony before the U.S. Senate Subcommittee on Communications in 1969.[2] At the time, Congress was considering reducing by half the Corporation for Public Broadcasting's request for $20 million of national funding. Senator John Pastore of Rhode Island, known as a straightforward, no-nonsense man who did not abide fools, opened the testimony somewhat crassly, saying, "All right, Rogers, you've got the floor."

Rogers unflinchingly began speaking in the same gentle, steady-paced, sing-song voice that could be heard on his television show—his authentic voice. He referred to a philosophical statement he had given the senator and said he trusted that the senator would read it as he had promised—that "one of the first things a child learns in a healthy family is trust."

The senator asked in a sarcastic tone, "Will it make you happy if you read it?"

Rogers responded, his pace and tone unchanged by the senator's sarcasm, "I'd just like to talk about it, if it's all right." He spoke briefly about the history of his program, commenting, "I'm very much concerned, as I know you are, about what's being delivered to our children in this country." He went on to say that children don't need to watch cartoons, which he described as "animated bombardment." The inner drama of growing up as a child is drama enough, he explained.

During that first minute and a half of Rogers' presentation, the senator set aside his gruffness and became genuinely curious.

Rogers continued, speaking about the importance of letting each child know that she is unique, and the value of conveying that "feelings are mentionable and manageable" for both the children's and the nation's mental health.

Pastore, now completely engaged, interjected, "I'm supposed to be a pretty tough guy, and this is the first time I've had goose bumps in the last two days."

Rogers, as unruffled by the praise as by the sarcasm, then asked the senator if he could share a song with him. The senator said, "Yes." Sitting in Congress at a time when America was entrenched in the Vietnam War, Rogers spoke the words to the song "What Do You Do with the Mad That You Feel," which ends with the lines:

> I can stop when I want to
> Can stop when I wish.
> I can stop, stop, stop any time.
> And what a good feeling to feel like this!
> And know that the feeling is really mine.
> Know that there's something deep inside
> That helps us become what we can.
> For a girl can be someday a lady
> And a boy can be someday a man.

Senator Pastore immediately replied, "I think it's wonderful, I think it's wonderful. Looks like you just earned the twenty million dollars." In less than seven minutes, the power of Rogers's authenticity had won over the crusty senator and garnered the funding for public television.

When a leader for the common good asks the question "Am I in the third circle?" in relation to the practice of gracious space, the question can become an invitation to remain true to his authentic self as he interacts with others. In addition, the question can remind the leader of the importance of inclusiveness: Am I daring enough to trust the power of gracious space in working for the common good, setting aside any doubts about its apparent softness? Am I ready to welcome the stranger? Am I as interested in other people's points of view as I am in my own? Can I welcome conflict and help the group move through it until it bears constructive fruit?

As a leader puts these practices to work, they become contagious. Group members begin to use them too, generating gracious space, the essential environment for cocreating the common good.

EXERCISES
Gracious Space / Self-Assessment

The following behaviors support the cocreation of gracious space. Circle those in which you feel competent. Put a star by those you could develop further. Then discuss with others or do some journaling about your strengths and what you would like to improve with respect to creating gracious space.[3]

- ★ Establishing norms
- ★ Interjecting humor/fun
- ★ Affirming others
- ★ Being open to feedback
- ★ Accepting of different perspectives and ideas
- ★ Innovating new approaches
- ★ Being present
- ★ Being aware of my impact on others
- ★ Assuming others' best intentions
- ★ Being intentional

* Being reliable
* Trusting others
* Being comfortable not knowing
* Detaching from outcomes
* Being collaborative
* Being trustworthy
* Being willing to change your mind
* Being willing to slow down
* Reflecting on assumptions
* Actively seek others' opinions
* Being curious
* Asking open-ended questions
* Discerning patterns emerging from group discussions
* Learning and sharing rather than just advocating
* Listening deeply
* Agreeing to be influenced
* Being comfortable receiving lots of questions
* Being capable of stopping, reassessing, and redirecting

REFLECTION QUESTIONS

* What is the current environment like in your group, community, or organization?

* Is it the kind of environment needed to advance your vision or other vital work of the group?

* What can you do to create gracious space for yourself each day?

* What kinds of people do you tend to distance yourself from, and how can you change your behavior to welcome them instead?

* What behaviors can you model to increase curiosity, risk-taking, and learning in public with your group, community, or organization?

* What can you do to discover and act as your authentic self?

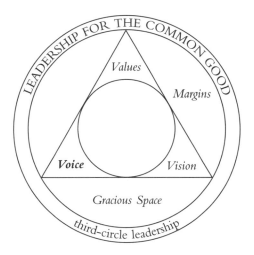

LEADERSHIP FOR THE COMMON GOOD

Values

Margins

Voice

Vision

Gracious Space

third-circle leadership

8 Claiming Your Voice

THE POET MARY OLIVER lives at the tip of Cape Cod, a realm of sea and forest that has served as her teacher and muse. From this place, she shows us through her poems what we miss as we drive to work in the morning or fill our evenings with television programs. Consider, she says in "The Fawn," what real holiness is through a chance encounter with a new-born deer on a Sunday morning. Listen, she suggests in "Wild Geese," to the invitation to authenticity in the cry of geese flying overhead.

Oliver discovered her voice early in life, once telling an interviewer, "I decided very early that I wanted to write. But I didn't think of it as a career. I didn't even think of it as a profession. . . . It was the most exciting thing, the most powerful thing, the most wonderful thing to do with my life. And I didn't question if I should—I just kept sharpening the pencils!"[1]

As a teenager and into her twenties, she lived for lengthy periods of time at Steepletop, the home of the deceased poet Edna St. Vincent Millay, a young companion to the poet's sister Norma Millay. She attended college for a while, but then she began expressing the poet's voice she had discovered and started to write.

She published her first poetry collection, *No Voyage, and Other Poems*, in 1963. Since then, she has published over a dozen collections of poems, plus several volumes of essays in which she frequently writes about the process of writing. She has received numerous awards, including the Pulitzer Prize, the National Book Award for Poetry, and the Lannan Literary Award.

In her poem "The Journey," Oliver describes the process of claiming our voice—stepping into action to do what we know we must do, despite our doubts and the critiques of others:

> One day you finally knew
> what you had to do, and began,
> though the voices around you
> kept shouting
> their bad advice—
> though the whole house
> began to tremble
> and you felt the old tug
> at your ankles.
> "Mend my life!"
> each voice cried.
> But you didn't stop.
> You knew what you had to do,
> though the wind pried
> with its stiff fingers
> at the very foundations—
> though their melancholy
> was terrible.
> It was already late
> enough, and a wild night,
> and the road full of fallen

branches and stones.
But little by little,
as you left their voices behind,
the stars began to burn
through the sheets of clouds,
and there was a new voice,
which you slowly
recognized as your own,
that kept you company
as you strode deeper and deeper
into the world,
determined to do
the only thing you could do—
determined to save
the only life you could save.[2]

Mary Oliver is a leader who exemplifies the process of claiming our voice and using it to work for the common good.

While a vision holds the promise of a preferred future, the promise is not enough to manifest that future. The vision needs to be put into action through the leader's voice. In this way, leaders exercise their commitment to the vision and become doers of their dream. Claiming voice is thus a critical step in the entire seven practices of common good leadership. Without voice, even the most finely crafted vision, grounded in principled values and holding the potential for furthering the common good, may never come into being because no one breathed life into it.

Voice refers not only to the words we use but to the full range of our behavior. Most people enjoy some modicum of intellectual, moral, economic, social, and political capital. How leaders choose to use these resources as well as other gifts defines the particular expression of their voice and the type of leadership they bring to the common good.

For artists such as Mary Oliver, their art form—whether it is writing, theater, film, dance, sculpture, painting, or music—becomes their voice to change our hearts and minds. In this way, artists engage in the type of leadership called "transforming leadership," discussed in chapter 3. Pablo Picasso painted the mural *Guernica* in response to the German and Italian warplanes bombing Basque country in 1937 and as a prophetic warning about the destructive power of modern technology. In his 1949 Pulitzer Prize-winning play, *Death of a Salesman,* Arthur Miller invited his audiences to take responsibility for their values before the world seduced them into focusing their lives on trifles. A decade later, folksinger Pete Seeger's "We Shall Overcome," his adaptation of a gospel song popular in black churches of the 1800s, stirred the hearts of nonviolent protesters not only in the U.S. Civil Rights Movement but in groups worldwide.

Voice imparts an emotional resonance in other forms as well. Martin Luther King Jr.'s voice manifested as compelling oratory. Thomas Jefferson's preferred mode of expression was highly crafted prose. Mahatma Gandhi touched the population of an entire subcontinent through his fasting and other acts of nonviolent protest. Harriet Tubman spoke with her feet as she led others to their freedom along the Underground Railroad.

The power to move and inspire others derives from the authenticity of the leader's voice. Whatever our vision may be, whatever action we are determined to undertake, our effectiveness as leaders is galvanized by our willingness to express our authentic selves.

Our voices as expressions of our authentic selves, are shaped by the totality of our life experiences. Yet our traumatic experiences as well as experiences of being marginalized seem to shape our voices the most, as illustrated by the following story. In December 1984, a thirteen-year-old hemophiliac named Ryan White was diagnosed with AIDS, having acquired the virus through a blood transfusion. This young teenager became the target of ill-informed fear-mongering, enduring threats of violence, social isolation from his peers at school, and homophobic epithets such as "We know you're queer" from people on the streets of his hometown.

Through these challenges, however, Ryan White found his voice. He became a spokesperson for the AIDS community, appearing on national television shows and participating in public benefits supporting children with AIDS until he died in March 1990, only a month short of his high school graduation. Four months later, Congress passed a bill to provide support for uninsured and underinsured AIDS patients, known as the Ryan White Care Act.

The importance of claiming our voice becomes evident when we consider what the world would be like if various leaders for the common good had not—for example, if Alexander Fleming had not pursued his vision of finding a wonder drug and discovered penicillin, or if the founders of the American experiment had never implemented their vision by writing the Bill of Rights. Whether our vision is big or small, we cannot know ahead of time the ripple effect that our voice may create, even long after we are gone. Thus claiming our voice, to act on our vision, may be of utmost significance to not only us but society and our common future.

THE PROCESS OF CLAIMING YOUR VOICE

For leaders for the common good, the process of claiming voice involves three steps: discovering their voice, expressing their voice, and using their voice to proclaim their vision. First, they discover their voice by determining which of many possible means of articulation suits them. Second, they express their voice by putting it to work—taking a stand on some concern and acting on it. Third, they use their voice to proclaim their specific vision for change. Whenever possible, leaders proclaim their vision in the conducive environment of gracious space, but sometimes advancing the vision requires presenting it in environments that are resistant or even hostile. Either way, by lending voice to their vision, leaders reveal it to a larger audience with the intent of making the world a better place.

Discovering Voice

Once leaders are committed to their vision, they must determine how they will express it by discovering their voice. The discovery of voice is directly related to finding a person's passion. Howard Thurman, author, theologian, and teacher who believed that connecting with our passion is the most important thing we can do for the world, stated, "Don't ask what the world needs. Ask what makes you come most alive, because what the world needs is people who have come alive."[3]

A sense of exhilaration is present when someone draws close to their passion. As Mary Oliver said about her writing, "It was the most exciting thing, the most powerful thing, the most wonderful thing to do with my life."

In this way, discovering voice is closely related to discovering vocation, the work we are called to do. Ideally our vocation is a blend of the work that fulfills us and the work that uses our unique talents for the betterment of the world.

Frederick Buechner, author and theologian, says in his book *Wishful Thinking: A Seeker's ABCs* that people discover their vocation at the intersection of their own great happiness—their passion—and the world's great need. When leaders discover voice at this intersection, they are in touch with not only their authentic selves but also their core values and their vision, and, through the vision, their experience of the margins.

How does a leader discover his voice at the intersection of his passion and the world's needs? One way is through engagement in the world. A teenager might discover a passion for teaching while working with young people at a summer camp. Mary Oliver confirmed her poet's voice by volunteering to help organize Ms. Millay's papers. Travel has opened the eyes of many to their passion and calling—Gandhi, Bono, and Princess Di were each deeply stirred by seeing unmet global needs firsthand.

Sometimes a person is led to his passion through his work. Vandana Shiva, trained as a scientist and now serving as a leader in the green movement in her native India and globally, found her vocation as a champion for change in global food production on a new job assignment. In an interview for the March 2002 issue of *Life Positive*, a magazine focused on holistic living, when the reporter asked Shiva when she made the switch from research to activism, she replied, "The Ministry of Environment invited me in 1981 to study the effect of mining in the Doon Valley. As a result of my report, the Supreme Court banned mining here in 1983. That was the first time I was doing something about conservation professionally. It was not just an analytic engagement divorced from action or consequences, and I found it so fulfilling to work with communities and make a difference to society . . . I cared enough about the environment to really see it saved, and I knew that research by itself would not do it."[47]

Other times a person is guided toward his passion through feedback from others combined with an honest assessment of their skills and talents. A parent might support a child's development of innate gifts in athletics, or a spouse might help a partner see that she enjoys working with the elderly more than accounting. Early in my career, I was drawn to the power and prestige of senior leadership roles in higher education, but by listening to feedback from colleagues and supervisors I eventually discovered I was a teacher and activist at heart.

In addition, a leader may discover his passion by observing someone else's calling. Seeing a doctor provide comfort in an emergency room, or a teacher touch the heart of a child, or an elected official sign a bill into law can introduce individuals to their own vocation.

Further, through meditation people can be guided by Spirit toward a vocation. When seeking discovery through meditation, it is helpful to have a trusted ally, or spiritual director, who can help us interpret the subtle messages of Spirit in the context of our vision and life.

Whether by these or other methods, the discovery of voice will happen for those who seek it. Leaders who have done the work of discovering their voice can then do their work in the world without fear of burnout. They are sustained by a passion that comes from the core of their being and the conviction that they are pursuing their true calling.

Expressing Voice

Once leaders discover their voice, the next step is expressing it. We express our voice by taking action, such as by stepping into our vocation as when a poet faces a blank page and actually writes, or when a teacher stands in front of a classroom for the first time and delivers a lesson. The key to taking this step is simply to begin, realizing that beginnings are never perfect. At first, expressing our voice might feel awkward and ineffective, like a child scratching out her first notes on the violin. Each time we practice expressing our voice, however, we gain in skill and confidence.

For a leader, taking action is about commitment to the vision—having the courage to give it energy, even before knowing whether it will be heralded or critiqued. Leaders expressing voice realize what they have to do and act on it.

The Scottish explorer W.H. Murray comments in his book about his expedition to the Himalayas:

Until one is committed, there is hesitancy, the chance to draw back, always ineffectiveness. Concerning all acts of initiative (and creation), there is one elementary truth the ignorance of which kills countless ideas and splendid plans: that the moment one definitely commits oneself, then providence moves too. A whole stream of events issues from the decision, raising in one's favor all manner of unforeseen incidents, meetings and material assistance, which no man could have dreamt would have come his way. I learned a deep respect for one of Goethe's couplets: "Whatever you can do or dream you can, begin it. Boldness has genius, power and magic in it!"[5]

Once we are committed and have crossed the threshold into action, everything shifts. Our dormant potential becomes activated, and another conscious voice is unleashed into the world. In addition, Spirit moves to greet those who venture forth, supporting their daring commitment through unfathomable coincidences that afford practical support. As a result of audacious actions and the fruitfulness of Spirit's generosity, the day comes closer when the common good worldview is fully established.

Expressing voice may mean taking a public stand about something that needs to be done to move our vision forward. For example, Martin Luther, sixteenth-century German leader of the Reformation, through long hours of contemplation, concluded that God must be a source of love and grace rather than the wielder of law and judgment as taught by the Church in his day. When he offered this insight to the world, he was not looking to be a change agent or a martyr. When the Church leaders challenged him to recant his teachings, however, he realized that he could not. He famously is attributed with saying, "Here I stand. I can do no other."[6]

Often expressing voice means taking action that others might be avoiding, such as raising an important yet difficult issue in an organization or community, even coordinating a meeting or rally to inspire group action. Taking such action includes addressing the practical details of when, where, and how to accomplish this. For example, if a rally is being planned it is necessary to figure out who will get the permit to march and who will alert the press.

When a leader expresses her voice, her own internal doubts as well as criticism from others are sure to show up. She may also feel thwarted by social and political influences, such as a narrow view of gender roles, expectations of professional decorum, or political oppression.

Sometimes internal questioning can inspire us to shift course slightly or critiques from others can be *good* advice. Determining when to listen to doubts and criticisms and when to listen to our personal passion, values, and vision involves third-circle choice-making. Yielding to critiques simply to please others belongs in the second circle of choice-making: "What will the neighbors think?" Authentic voice, on the other hand, puts down roots in the third circle, where leaders are guided by principle and a commitment to what is good for all.

Leaders for the common good express their voice boldly but not with rigid devotion. Grounded in the third circle, they become like willow trees deeply rooted in soil. They can take a solid stand but also remain flexible, able to bend in response to new information that may assist them in further refining their vision and purpose as they move into action.

Using Voice to Proclaim the Vision

Once leaders have discovered and expressed their voice, they use it to publicly proclaim their vision of a specific change in a particular corner of the world. What a leader does when proclaiming her vision is summed up in the phrase "speak the truth in love to power," popularized by professor and activist Cornel West. This phrase, which has been the hallmark for many action strategies to advance justice, offers a bare-bones formula for proclaiming a vision through voice in ways that model the common good.

First, using voice to proclaim a vision means publicly *speaking the truth* of that vision. The vision's truth is contained in the three elements of its inception: the problem that needs addressing (what is), the moral and other reasons why a change is needed (what ought to be), and the change that offers the solution (what could be). It is natural to begin with naming the problem—describing what is. Publicly declaring an injustice casts the light of collective awareness on it, calling the injustice out of hiding, putting the perpetuators on notice, and pointing out the costs of blindly clinging to the status quo. Thomas Hardy, English poet and author, said, "If way to the Better there be, it exacts a full look at the Worst."[7] Often being made aware of a situation of suffering, limitation, or lack is enough to convince listeners to join the effort for change.

For example, Upton Sinclair wrote *The Jungle* in 1906 to expose the inhumane working conditions in the U.S. meat-packing industry. For seven weeks he worked undercover in the industry and reported on the gruesome conditions his fellow workers endured on a daily basis. His informed descriptions exposed these appalling practices to the light of day, leading to government regulation of the food industry.

Stating the moral and other reasons for a change highlights the gap between what ought to be and what is. Listeners not motivated by the problem alone may find the moral argument, the "oughtness" of the situation, serving as their wake-up call.

Finally, giving voice to a change that offers a solution—what could be—stirs the imagination of those in the community who enjoy bringing the possible into reality. Together, these three acts of truth-telling lay out the vision for others to see.

Second, the truth should be spoken *in love*. When leaders take action to bring about change, the natural response is to perceive anyone who resists such change, especially those in power, as malevolent. It is especially difficult to remember love when we experience the power of the opposition and our instincts urge us to fight back. Thus it is all too easy for reform leaders to slip into the very us–them mentality that perpetuates the problem they hope to address. Special attention is required to engage the opposition from a standpoint of love. Love is the force that moves us past the divisiveness of us–them thinking and into the inclusiveness of the third circle, where work for the common good can be done. According to poet Edwin Markham, cited on page 36, we draw the opposition into the third circle with us.

Michael Edwards, a senior fellow at Demos, a public policy institute, describes love as "active, not passive, explicitly considering the effects of oppressive and exploitative systems and structures on the welfare of others, and not just focused on the immediate circle of family and friends—a deep and abiding commitment to the liberation of all."[8] The goal of speaking the truth in love, then, is to advance change in a system while maintaining respect for those who are a part of the system, convincing them to halt the wrongdoing by reminding them of their own capacity for compassion and goodness.

Seeking justice with love becomes a social force that transforms both systems and the hearts of those who hold power in the systems. Mahatma Gandhi called this force, which was the driving principle behind India's nonviolent movement for independence, *satyagraha*, literally, "truth force." Martin Luther King Jr., having studied the nonviolent practices of Gandhi, integrated these teachings into his own work, calling it "soul force." He believed nonviolence to be the most powerful force on earth because it has the power to turn an enemy into a friend.

A stunning example of the power of soul force in addressing injustices is seen in the life of the late George Wallace, who as governor of Alabama during the Civil Rights Movement was a vigilant guardian of segregation. Later in his life, while campaigning for the presidency, he was shot by a white man and spent the rest of his life wracked with pain and confined to a wheelchair. His personal suffering opened his eyes and heart to the suffering of others and inspired him to embrace inclusiveness.

On March 10, 1995, the thirtieth anniversary of the Selma-to-Montgomery civil rights march, a repentant George Wallace arrived at the celebration to show his support. Joseph Lowery, one of the black organizers of the event, offered these words as greeting: "You are a different George Wallace today. We both serve a God who can make the desert bloom. We ask God's blessing on you."[9]

Wallace told those in the crowd who had marched thirty years earlier: "Much has transpired since those days. A great deal has been lost and a great deal gained, and here we are. My message to you today is, welcome to Montgomery. May your message be heard. May your lessons never be forgotten."[10]

Opportunities to engage an unjust system in love are available everywhere. We all live and work within systems, structures, and institutions. Most of them do not have an evil intent, yet all of them are capable of doing harm. Corporations strategically keep employee hours under forty per week so that they do not have to pay benefits. Police departments engage in unconscious racial profiling. Neighbors use chemicals on their lawns not realizing that the runoff is polluting a nearby lake. Children are bullied on school playgrounds. A gas station does not dispose of used oil properly. Or a supervisor mistreats women.

Each of these scenarios creates an opportunity for a leader to practice using her voice to proclaim her vision of what could be. Always the goal is to not only speak the truth but to do so in love. And it is not always necessary to act alone; other concerned people—parents, neighbors, coworkers—are often willing to use their voices to support a vision.

Third, speaking the truth in love is most effective when addressed *to power*, to those holding the reins in the system perpetuating the status quo. While it may be easier to talk about the system's failings with peers than to speak directly to supervisors or bosses, talking about those in power in the parking lot or at the water cooler is not likely to bring about the needed transformation. Yet many individuals stop short of addressing those in power directly because it can be dangerous. People in institutions who speak unwelcome truths, even if they do so in love, risk being branded as troublemakers, and troublemakers are often not promoted and might eventually be terminated. Community change agents similarly risk being denigrated or having their demands denied.

When speaking directly to power, leaders for the common good engage all four cornerstones of leadership for the common good: justice, care, inclusiveness, and moral urgency. Committed to justice and the fierce urgency of now, they seek immediate change in the system. They articulate clear demands and explain the lengths to which the disenfranchised are willing to go to achieve change. As those in power see that their current path is more costly than risking reform, whether economically, politically, or personally, they eventually comply willingly with the interests of the people. Committed to care and inclusiveness, leaders aim not to belittle the authority of those in power but rather allow them to assume a principled orientation to the world while saving face. Such an invitation to a third-circle orientation awakens the moral sense of the resistance.

While speaking the truth directly to those in power can effectively advance social change, sometimes bringing change to the system doesn't require it. Some leaders for the common good simply innovate, creating change regardless of the people in power, thus speaking to power more indirectly. For example, when the banks would not set up loans for poor village women, Muhammad Yunus gave out loans himself and eventually created an entirely new kind of bank designed for microlending. The decision to circumnavigate power can also be seen in the recent green and organic movements, which effect change largely at the grassroots level. In response, those in power *must* move in the new direction people have chosen, often running to keep up with the reform, if only to maintain market share or get reelected.

Finally, sometimes we ourselves are the people in power who resist change. We may know global warming is happening yet still drive our cars whenever we want. We may realize the need for less divisive politics yet disparage those on the other side of "the aisle." We may be fully aware of ecological concerns yet still use plastic bags from the grocery store. As Walt Kelly's comic strip character Pogo famously said, "We have met the enemy, and he is us." Difficult as it is, we also need to speak the truth in love to ourselves.

The key question for a leader for the common good, "Am I in the third circle?" takes on new aspects when his intention is to claim his voice. While considering how to express his voice—what actions to take—the question "Am I in the third circle?" becomes "Are my intentions good, clear, and in line with my vision?" While engaging in action, the question may mean: Am I speaking the truth rather than wavering from it because of internal or external pressures? Am I committed to engaging those in a position to make a difference? Am I able to approach power while maintaining love in my heart? Am I able to invite the status quo into the third circle?

What if all people were inspired to claim their voice? Imagine a land where all people are inspired to claim their voice and do so with authenticity and moral clarity. Each voice discovered, expressed, and used to proclaim a vision for the common good has great power; like a river that shapes deep canyons or broad fertile plains, it can shape the future. When these voices flow together, the resulting confluence is a movement for the common good whose power is irresistible.

EXERCISES

Discovering Your Voice

Discovering your voice can take the form of reflection on questions that have the power to stir you. The following questions are a starting place for meditation to discover your voice and vocation.

* If you knew you could not fail, what would you be willing to try?
* What work do you find enthralling? What could happen in five to ten years if you continued doing that work?
* What legacy do you want to leave behind?
* What work of justice are you utterly convinced needs to be accomplished in the next decade?
* What global need captures your heart? What creative response can you imagine leading?
* What do you want to say to the world with your life?
* What work makes you happy?

Expressing Your Voice and Proclaiming a Vision

Step One

Identify a concern you feel passionate about and do one of the following:

* Write a letter to the editor of your local or campus newspaper.
* Prepare an outline for a speech you could present to an individual or group in a position to make a difference if persuaded by what you say.
* Write a poem, song, or short story that expresses your passionate concern.
* Start a group or a movement that will give collective voice to your passion.
* Think of a creative act of nonviolent civil disobedience that will draw attention to your concern.

★ Consider doing an end run around the status quo and innovate a new creative alternative to satisfy your passion.

Step Two

Gather with one or two close friends and share one of the ideas listed above, asking for constructive feedback.

Step Three

Perform three actions to take your voice public.

O

REFLECTION QUESTIONS

★ What is your passion?

★ Who or what is giving you bad advice and asking you to play it safe?

★ What will inspire you to move past the voices that would keep you from fully claiming your voice?

★ What first three steps could you take?

★ Of those three steps, which one will you take today?

★ What can you do to ensure that your voice is and remains nonviolent?

9 Receiving Hope

MARTIN LUTHER KING JR., born in 1929 in Atlanta, Georgia, grew up just a few houses away from Ebenezer Baptist Church, where his father served as pastor. By age twenty-six, he had completed college and seminary training, been ordained a Baptist minister, married, and earned a doctorate in systematic theology.

The natural course for Dr. King would have been to eventually take his father's place as lead pastor at Ebenezer Baptist Church. His life took a different path, however. Returning to the South in 1955, he accepted the pastorate of Dexter Avenue Baptist Church in Montgomery, Alabama. That year Rosa Parks was arrested for refusing to give up her seat on a Montgomery City bus to a white man. When the black community chose King to head the Montgomery Improvement Association, he helped organize the bus boycott that eventually launched the Civil Rights Movement and his career as its leader.

One of King's darkest moments, and a turning point in his life, came soon after the 381-day boycott started. On January 26, 1956, King, having been arrested and jailed, returned home just in time to receive one more in a series of threatening phone calls. Worried about his safety and that of his wife and baby daughter, he sat alone shortly before midnight filled with fear and despair over a cup of coffee. He described that moment many years later in a sermon:

> I got to the point that I couldn't take it any longer. I was weak. Something said to me, "You can't call on Daddy now, You can't even call on Mama now. You've got to call on that something that your Daddy used to tell you about. That power that can make a way out of no way."
>
> In this midnight hour, religion had become real to me and I had to know God for myself. With my head in my hands, I bowed down over that cup of coffee. Oh yes, I prayed a prayer. I prayed out loud that night. The words that I spoke to God that midnight are still vivid in my memory: "Lord, I'm down here trying to do what's right. I think I'm right. I think the cause we represent is right. But Lord I must confess that I am weak now, I am faltering. I'm losing my courage. I am afraid. . . . I am at the end of my powers."
>
> At that moment, I experienced the presence of the Divine as I had never experienced him before. I could hear an inner voice saying to me, "Martin Luther, stand up for righteousness, stand up for justice, stand up for truth. And lo I will be with you even until the end of the world."[1]

From that day forward, although still haunted by fear, he was no longer a victim of despair. His experience with God that night had gifted him with hope that saw him through everything to come. Knowing beyond a shadow of a doubt that his cause was right, he marched into fire hoses, police dogs, state patrol on horseback, truncheons, and rifles while adhering to methods of nonviolence. He spent a good deal of time in dusty jail cells while the stream of hate mail and death threats continued. He endured the critiques of racists and cautious clergy alike, and was even stabbed by a mentally disturbed black woman during a book signing in Harlem before finally being assassinated in 1968. Martin Luther King Jr. is a leader who exemplifies trusting that hope will arrive in the most challenging moments of working for the common good.

As leaders for the common good proclaim their vision and begin working to implement it, they experience periods of confidence and progress offset by times of anguish during setbacks, when they are in need of hope, the attribute most capable of facing down despair. Joan Chittister, Benedictine author and activist, says, "When tragedy strikes, when trouble comes, when life disappoints us, we stand at the crossroads between hope and despair, torn and hurting. Despair cements us in the present; hope sends us dancing around dark corners trusting in a tomorrow we cannot see."[2] The way to the common good is not always paved and at times no more than a rough track that can seem to disappear altogether. Hope finds us in the thick of things. With hope, leaders can continue their work for the common good even when circumstances suggest all is lost.

At times, hope is confused with optimism—the expectation that things are going to turn out the way we wish. We say, "I hope the Red Sox win" or "I hope she calls again." But hope in the context of common good leadership has more muscle than optimism. As poet Vaclav Havel, social reformer and former president of Czechoslovakia, explains, "Hope is definitely not the same thing as optimism. Hope is not the conviction that something will turn out well, but the certainty that something makes sense, regardless of how it turns out."[3]

To express this fuller meaning, the word *hope* almost needs an adjective, such as *deep,* similar to "deep ecology." "Deep hope" hints at a more profound nature of hope than a casual mention of the word usually implies—the form of hope that leadership for the common good requires.

Leadership for the common good invites leaders to face the challenges of the day trusting that hope will appear and a way will be shown. The counterintuitive advice to leaders is not to escape into denial but to stay and work, to walk directly into the challenge, and the despair and fear that accompany it, believing it is in these dark moments that we are most likely to encounter hope.

HOPE AS A GIFT OF LIGHT IN THE DARKNESS

While the other six elements in the common good leadership model are developed through practice, hope can only be received like a welcome gift. As the poet Emily Dickinson points out, hope simply arrives, like a bird, without asking anything of us:

> *"Hope" is the thing with feathers—*
> *That perches in the soul—*
> *And sings the tune without the words—*
> *And never stops—at all—*
>
> *. . . . .*
>
> *I've heard it in the chillest land—*
> *And on the strangest Sea—*
> *Yet—never—in Extremity,*
> *It asked a crumb—of me.*[4]

Because hope comes from a transcendent source, where the winds of doubt and fear have no access, it can meet any difficulty life presents. It also offers a window onto this transcendent realm, which existed before time and space. As such, hope is preexistent and eternal. When we receive hope, we know it is a gift from a transcendent realm and it offers strength to help us meet any difficulty that life presents. Once the spark of hope is lit in a leader's heart, it will never be snuffed out by forces of the status quo, even if the leader is swallowed into the belly of despair. Nor can the gift of hope be repaid. Our only task is to receive this gift with gratitude and put it to use while getting on with the business of advancing the common good.

For many leaders, such as Martin Luther King Jr., Sojourner Truth, and St. Francis of Assisi, hope comes through an encounter with Spirit. Hope does not call for a religious orientation, however. Vaclav Havel did not follow a religion, yet he did observe that hope arrives from somewhere outside of ourselves and beyond our own resources. He commented, "I think that the deepest and most important form of hope, the only one that can keep us above water and urge us to good works, and the only true source of the breathtaking dimension of the human spirit and its efforts, is something we get, as it were, from 'elsewhere.'"[5] Because encounters with hope cannot be created or controlled, the only thing leaders can do to receive hope is to move into the territory where hope is likely to arrive. In Dickinson's imagery of hope as a bird, engaging with hope is a bit like going on a bird-watching hike. An experienced backcountry guide, when asked by a novice, "Are we going to see eagles today?" responds, "I plan to take us to places where we are most likely to see them, but whether or not they appear is up to the eagles."

The territory where we are likely to encounter hope is on the classic hero's journey. In countless versions of the journey, the hero must leave behind familiar settings to move into the adventure. For instance, in *Star Wars* Luke Skywalker bids farewell to life on his home planet, Tatooine. Similarly, in *The Fellowship of the Ring* Frodo and Sam leave behind the comforting rhythms of life in the Shire. While walking through a gorgeous meadow not far from home, Sam halts, turns to Frodo, and says, "If I take one more step, it'll be the farthest away from home I've ever been."[6]

Not long after, joined by two companions they are chased through the dark woods by a Nazgul, one of the evil agents of Lord Sauron, till they huddle for safety under the cut bank of a river. It is here, surrounded by danger, that the Hobbits' adventure begins.

Our natural human response is to avoid difficulty and stay in the safety of the meadow—ask safe meadow questions, make safe meadow plans, and dream safe meadow dreams. But as Tolkien points out, change for the better rarely happens that way. Likewise, a poster in a college friend's dorm room portrays a photograph of a tall sailing ship moored quietly in a harbor has a caption that reads, "Ships are safe in a harbor, but that's not what ships are made for."

Walking into the difficulties on our watch may not be easy, but these formidable places often mark the territory of leadership for the common good, and they are frequently where leaders receive hope enough to act. For example, in June 1939, during the Nazi era, Dietrich Bonhoeffer, German theologian and martyr, was invited to return to the Union Theological Seminary in New York, where he had done postgraduate work a decade earlier. He accepted the invitation for fear of being conscripted by the Nazi regime. As a committed pacifist, he could not endure the thought of being connected to Hitler's abhorrent vision.

Later that year, however, after wrestling with his conscience, Bonhoeffer decided to leave his comfortable position at the university and return to Germany to serve in the resistance to the Nazi regime. Explaining his rationale in a letter to Reinhold Niebuhr, his colleague and mentor at Union, he said: "I have come to the conclusion that I made a mistake in coming to America. I must live through this difficult period in our national history with the people of Germany. I will have no right to participate in the reconstruction of Christian life in Germany after the war if I do not share the trials of this time with my people."[7]

Subsequently, in Germany Bonhoeffer served as a double agent, working within the Nazi regime and as a courier for the

German resistance movement. He was eventually discovered, arrested, and then executed at Flossenburg concentration camp in April 1945, only weeks before the Soviet army entered Berlin.

As leaders face their most difficult issues, doubts are likely to arise in their minds, and they may feel interrogated by self-doubt: This issue has been around so long, what makes me think I can make a difference? With the resistance our culture has placed around such hot-button issues, what makes me think I have the right and power to tackle this problem in our community? Questions like these or other trials accompany most journeys toward the creation of a more just and caring world. Hope says keep coming.

When hope appears in the midst of such darkness and doubt, the nature of the problem is transformed from something overwhelming into something that, although challenging, appears surmountable. Questions may remain but are no longer debilitating. The cultural resistance may continue, though it is no longer unbearable.

Stewart Burns, historian and Martin Luther King Jr. scholar, gives us a picture of how hope meets and empowers us in the most difficult moments. Describing Dr. King's response to his encounter with despair after his family was threatened, Burns noted: "He clung to his faith, however, that the divine force was buried in the deepest darkness. That if he carried his candle of faith deeper and still deeper into the heart of darkness, the darkness at the heart of life, he would discover the blinding light at the Center of God's creation, the fire at the core of his own soul."[8]

One of the most moving demonstrations of the light of hope shining in the darkness is told by Elie Wiesel in *Night*, his autobiographical recounting of the horror of the Holocaust. At the end of World War II, in a last desperate attempt to kill Jews, the SS guards led hundreds of men on a fifty-mile march at night in the dead of winter. At the end of this death march, the men who survived were crowded into a decaying building where, exhausted, some began to sleep. It was so crowded that people were lying on top of one another, in some cases several bodies deep. Wiesel, who was fifteen at the time, describes someone lying on top of him, covering his face such that he could not breathe. Fortunately he managed to forge a hole through the layers of dying people so he could get just enough air to avoid suffocation.

In the midst of this living nightmare, one of Wiesel's childhood friends, Juliek, made a radical choice. Wiesel reports: "I heard the sound of a violin. The sound of a violin in this dark shed, where the dead were heaped on the living. . . . It must have been Juliek. He played a fragment from Beethoven's concerto. I have never heard sounds so pure. In such a silence. It was pitch dark. I could hear only the violin and it was as though Juliek's soul were the bow."[9]

HOPE'S GIFTS TO LEADERSHIP

Once hope arrives, it does not change the truth of what is or lessen the difficulties of shifting to what ought to be. But it does help leaders perceive possibility where none seemed to exist.

I became aware of a poignant metaphor for this shift in perception one midsummer Saturday afternoon some years ago when I was doing some friendly wrestling on the backyard lawn with my sons Nic and Ben, ages eight and seven. We tumbled across the lawn toward a row of rose bushes planted along its edge. Staring up into the intricate branches, I saw there were about two hundred thorns and only three roses. I suddenly realized that focusing on the roses among the sea of thorns was like receiving hope amidst difficulty, an experience that caused my mind to shift to a positive perspective.

Like seeing the roses amidst the many thorns, glimpsing hope invites people not to lose sight of the possibilities for a better future seeded in a vision despite the challenges before them. Hope offers a balanced view. If leaders pretend there are no thorns, they and others may be hurt when they brush up against them. If leaders can see only thorns and no roses, they may lose sight of their vision of what could be and risk cynicism and continuation of the status quo.

Acknowledging the thorns yet receiving hope from the roses has stood humanity in good stead time after time. For example, when President Abraham Lincoln dedicated the National Cemetery at Gettysburg in November 1863, four months after the battle at Gettysburg had resulted in the death of more soldiers than any other Civil War battle, he was fully aware of the devastation linked to the setting but nevertheless pointed to the rose—the unfinished promise of the American experiment in democracy—to give hope and support his sense of purpose:

> It is for us the living, rather, to be dedicated here to the unfinished work which they who fought here have thus far so nobly advanced. It is rather for us to be here dedicated to the great task remaining before us—that from these honored dead we take increased devotion to that cause for which they gave the last full measure of devotion—that we here highly resolve that these dead shall not have died in vain—that this nation, under God, shall have a new birth of freedom—and that government of the people, by the people, for the people, shall not perish from the earth.[10]

Similarly in 1940, as England prepared to face the brunt of Hitler's aggression on the western front, Winston Churchill, speaking before the House of Commons, focused the country's attention on its own tenacity and courage:

> The whole fury and might of the enemy must very soon be turned on us. Hitler knows that he will have to break us in this Island or lose the war. If we can stand up to him, all Europe

may be free and the life of the world may move forward into broad, sunlit uplands. But if we fail, then the whole world, including the United States, including all that we have known and cared for, will sink into the abyss of a new Dark Age made more sinister, and perhaps more protracted, by the lights of perverted science. Let us therefore brace ourselves to our duties, and so bear ourselves that, if the British Empire and its Commonwealth last for a thousand years, men will still say, "This was their finest hour."[11]

The capacity to shift perspective to see hope and possibility empowers leaders to make radical choices for the good. Radical choices may appear to defy logic and prudence, but the voice of hope—the often intuitive voice that says, "In spite of the evidence, believe"—can encourage leaders to make radical choices despite apparent difficulties.

For example, a Native American woman decided to start an Alcoholics Anonymous group on her reservation. She advertised the first meeting, but no one came and she sat alone at the meeting venue the entire allotted time. The next week, she advertised the meeting again. Again no one showed up. With an eye on the potential good an Alcoholics Anonymous program could bring to her people, she continued announcing the meeting week after week and waiting with hope. Finally, after nine months had passed, one person joined her. Then another. Over the next five years more people came, and the group flourished, becoming an asset to the community.

Another example of hope empowering a radical choice is in the words of the song "Lift Every Voice and Sing," written by James Weldon Johnson in 1899, which many black Americans regard as their national anthem because it describes their experience in America. One stanza in particular makes the point:

Stony the road we trod, bitter the chastening rod,
Felt in the days when hope unborn had died;
Yet with a steady beat, have not our weary feet,
Come to the place for which our fathers sighed?[12]

The first two lines bear witness to the black experience in America, riddled as it is with injustice and pain. The simple word *yet*, on which the stanza hinges, testifies to the power of hope, and the two lines that follow express a radical choice for hope inspired by Spirit.

The gift of hope can also be generative. A single well-timed and courageously conceived act by a leader that inspires hope can start a movement that changes history, as illustrated by the following story.

Jan Stary, a professional photographer and a friend of mine, was one of the thousands of Czechs who on a cold November day in 1989 gathered in Wenceslas Square in Prague to protest the Soviet-backed communist regime. Someone in the crowd began to shake his keys as a sign of the hope-inspired protest, and in just a few days, the number of key shakers grew quickly to an estimated half million. All of the protestors were at risk of enduring a brutal backlash from the forces of the Soviet army. Yet they stood together in the November frost with the belief that their collective nonviolent voice had the political power to convince the communist regime to step down. Two weeks later, the leaders of the protest organized a work strike throughout Czechoslovakia, which ushered in the Velvet Revolution and a new era of democracy for the Czech people.

Similarly, Wangari Maathai, a Kenyan scientist, activist, and Nobel Prize winner for her work in bringing sustainable environmental and democratic practices to Africa, became aware of the rapid deforestation in Africa. As a response, on World Environment Day in 1977 she helped organize the planting of seven trees at a public park in Kenya's capital, Nairobi. This small act, inspired by the hope to one day see Africa full of trees again, stirred the same hope in others. It grew into the Green Belt Movement, in which village women began protecting the environment and helping their families while being paid for planting trees. Since its founding, the movement has planted millions of trees in Kenya and other African countries.

In such cases, hope-inspired action becomes contagious among people interested in acting for the common good. Norman Cousins points out, "The capacity for hope is the most significant fact of life. It provides human beings with a sense of destination and the energy to get started."[13]

PRACTICES FOR INVITING HOPE

Although hope comes as a gift and cannot be developed, engaging in the following practices invites the gift because they move the leader into the demanding territory essential for advancing the common good.

Begin

Beginning to act summons hope. I learned this for the first time at age ten when, after an astounding three feet of snow had fallen during one night in the Massachusetts town where I grew up, my older brothers pointed out that it was my turn to shovel the front sidewalk. I remember standing with the shovel in snow as high as the middle of my ribs, looking from one end of the twenty-foot distance to the other and feeling tempted to just give up and go inside. Then something inside me said quietly, "Why not give it a try?"

Next, I made a plan: I would dig a narrow trough one shovel's width wide down to the cement along the center of the entire twenty-foot length. Each time my shovel hit the cement sidewalk,

I gained hope and encouragement. Finally, I broke through at the far end. Widening the path would obviously take far longer than cutting that first swath, but by that time I was infused with energy and with certainty that I could finish.

Most of us face daunting tasks at times and have to somehow find the capacity to act. For example, farmers facing the empty fields of spring consider the hard work ahead before fall harvest. Single mothers look into the eyes of their infants and wonder where they'll find the strength to raise a child alone. All great works begin the same way: with some single action that invites hope.

Walk into the Difficult Issues and Keep Going

To invite hope, it helps if leaders are willing to take an honest look at the difficult truths of social situations and ask their contemporaries to do the same. For example, Martin Luther King Jr. plumbed the ugly depths of American racism and asked all Americans to make an equally honest assessment of the moral state of the union. Former Vice President Al Gore took a hard look at the inconvenient truth of global warming and asked people throughout the world to confront the same difficult issue. The Dalai Lama met the Tibetan people's suffering with honesty and compassion, making his mere presence a reminder of the immoral nature of the Chinese government's oppression of his people.

The Alcoholics Anonymous (AA) community understands the value of looking at difficult truths in order to make peoples' lives better. In AA's programs, recovery begins with individuals declaring the difficult truth that they are alcoholics. Those in recovery know that healing requires commitment to truth-telling about challenging questions and that hope emerges on the other side of their decision to face the difficult truth. AA has much to teach leaders about walking right into the challenges on their watch—speaking the truth in love about the plight of those on the margins in their communities and the changes being promoted. Like those in recovery, such leaders can expect that, with diligence and the support hope offers, they will be able to keep their vision alive despite challenges and resistance from others. Winston Churchill once advised, "If you are going through hell, keep going."[14] When engaging with difficult truths, difficult questions, or difficult people becomes a habit, there is great reason to believe change for the good of all will happen.

Remember

To invite hope, it helps if leaders remember similar difficult situations when hope arrived. Perhaps no institution practices memory as a means to summon hope more powerfully than the American Black Church, which believes in a God of hope who helps those trapped in despair to find "a way out of no way"—an African American folk saying serving as a reminder that hope is always possible. The American Black Church's hope is sustained by memory—that of their own and their forebearers' suffering, which keeps them alert to present-day injustices, and the memory of Spirit's faithfulness, which allows them to plan for the future. In large part, the work of Martin Luther King Jr. was to assist other blacks in recalling their strength, power, dignity, and their God, who would once again help them find a way. Their main job was to keep protesting and singing, trusting that their actions would summon the power of Spirit to sustain them with hope while they worked to transform the status quo and advance the common good.

In the Jewish tradition, Passover, which centers on the memory of the Jews finding their way out of bondage and oppression by following the call of Spirit, likewise ushers in hope. A further valuable practice for leaders is to inspire others to remember and share their own stories of hope coming to them during difficult circumstances. In telling stories of hope, we recycle the original gift of hope, extending Spirit's generosity to new times and places.

Believe

Perhaps the primary way leaders can invite hope is by believing that Spirit is trustworthy and they will receive hope. Belief creates expectancy and gives us eyes for seeing hope when it arrives. Belief also makes us more likely to recognize the hope already around us in the form of resources, allies, and opportunities needed to work for the common good in various situations.

During his Nobel Peace Prize acceptance speech on December 10, 1964, nearly a decade after his midnight encounter with hope, Martin Luther King Jr. spoke of the belief—the "audacious faith"—that kept him moving forward, and encouraged us all to move forward with him, in the company of hope, toward a better future:

> I accept this award today with an abiding faith in America and an audacious faith in the future of mankind. I refuse to accept despair as the final response to the ambiguities of history. I refuse to accept the idea that the "is-ness" of man's present nature makes him morally incapable of reaching up for the eternal "ought-ness" that forever confronts him. I refuse to accept the idea that man is mere flotsam and jetsam in the river of life, unable to influence the unfolding events which surround him. I refuse to accept the view that mankind is so tragically bound to the starless midnight of racism and war that the bright daybreak of peace and brotherhood can never become a reality.
>
> I refuse to accept the cynical notion that nation after nation must spiral down a militaristic stairway into the hell of thermonuclear destruction. I believe that unarmed truth and unconditional love will have the final word in reality. This is why right, temporarily defeated, is stronger than evil triumphant. . . . I have the audacity to believe that peoples everywhere can have three meals a day for their bodies, education and culture for their minds, and dignity, equality, and

freedom for their spirits. I believe that what self-centered men
have torn down, men other-centered can build up. . . . I still
believe that we shall overcome.[15]

Spirit asks us to walk together into the remaining difficult work of
social justice and trust that hope will meet us there.

EXERCISES

Opening Ourselves to Hope

To feel confident walking into the difficulties on your watch
trusting that hope will find you, consider the following scenarios.
Before beginning, think of an actual social injustice or problem that
concerns you.

Scenario One

Over the past decade, you have engaged the social ill and
have expressed your concerns at neighborhood meetings, written
an editorial, and even given testimony at the city council. On each
occasion you decided, for the sake of decorum, to ask polite questions and propose reasonable alternatives. Not much change happened throughout this period of time, though people praised you
for raising such good questions in a responsible fashion.

Scenario Two

At first you engaged the social concern in a polite manner,
but little changed. Realizing that your response to the question
"Am I in the third circle?" was no, you decided to express the concern with greater moral clarity and conviction. Your public questions pushed the envelope of accepted norms and made your peers
uncomfortable. In response, your neighbors invited you to fewer
potlucks and game nights, causing you on occasion to feel isolated

and alone in your own hometown. Yet during the next decade, you became increasingly more informed on the issue and, hearing the voice of hope encouraging you forward, you raised more difficult questions with neighbors, the media, and the city council. As a result, a few people joined you and modest progress occurred regarding your cause.

Which scenario do you prefer? Why?

REFLECTION QUESTIONS

* Does pursuing the vision you articulated in chapter 6 require you to encounter difficult questions or circumstances?

* If so, how will you prepare yourself to leave the safe places and walk into the darkness?

* Do you believe hope will find you? Why, or why not?

* Recall a time when things looked dark yet hope arrived. What attitudes may have invited hope?

* How can you help others find hope?

10 Acting with Courage

THE BURMESE SOCIAL ACTIVIST Aung San Suu Kyi, born in 1945, was shaped by her parents' participation in civic and governmental affairs. Her father, Aung San, assassinated when she was two years old, was regarded as the father of modern-day Burma. Her mother, Daw Khin Kyi, raised Suu Kyi and her two brothers to be deeply committed to Buddhist practice and civic responsibilities. When Suu Kyi was fifteen, her mother was appointed the ambassador to India, and the family moved to India, where Suu Kyi was introduced to the principles of nonviolent resistance.

After earning a bachelor's degree at Oxford University and working for three years at the United Nations in New York City, Suu Kyi married fellow Oxford student Michael Aris in 1972 and settled in England. However, in April 1988 Suu Kyi's mother became ill, and Suu Kyi returned to Burma to care for her. Back in her homeland, Suu Kyi soon became the leader of the popular nationwide democracy movement. She wrote an open letter to the military junta controlling the country, asking them to cease using arms against peaceful, un-armed protesters and to return political power to the people.

During the protests that followed, more than ten thousand demonstrators were killed. Despite the ban on large political gatherings, Suu Kyi traveled the country giving speeches before large crowds, although she was harassed by the military. A writer reports on her striking demonstration of courage: "In one town as she was walking down the street with her associates, soldiers lined up in front of her with their rifles at the ready, threatening to shoot if she advanced any further. She calmly walked on and at the last moment a higher officer countermanded the order to fire."[1] Her campaign unified the opposition to the government and also introduced human rights and the principles of nonviolence as goals closely related to the tenets of Buddhism.

In 1989, Suu Kyi was placed under house arrest. Even so, the pro-democracy movement grew so strong that in 1990 the military junta announced a general election. Suu Kyi won an extraordinary 82 percent of the vote, making her the country's prime minister. The junta, however, refused to recognize the election results and soon cut off her communication with her family in England, evidently to break her spirit.

Since then she has spent the majority of her time under house arrest and endured mixed messages and harassment from the junta. In 1997, her husband, still living in England, was diagnosed with terminal cancer and wanted to visit Suu Kyi. The government of Burma, by then renamed Myanmar, refused him a visa but told Suu Kyi she could visit him and their two children in England. Knowing that once she left the country she would not be able to return, she decided to stay in Myanmar.

In her acceptance message for the 1990 Sakharov Prize for Freedom of Thought, she bore witness to the resilience of courage in the face of one of the most oppressive fear-based regimes:

Within a system, which denies the existence of basic human rights, fear tends to be the order of the day. Fear of imprisonment, fear of torture, fear of death, fear of losing friends, family, property or means of livelihood, fear of poverty, fear of isolation, fear of failure. . . . It is not easy for a people conditioned by fear under the iron rule of the principle that might is right to free themselves from the enervating miasma of fear. Yet even under the most crushing state machinery courage rises up again and again, for fear is not the natural state of civilized man.[2]

Finally, on November 13, 2010, Suu Kyi was released from house arrest, after being detained fifteen of the twenty-one preceding years. She has received numerous international awards, including the Nobel Peace Prize, the Sakharov Prize, and the U.S. Medal of Freedom. She is a leader who exemplifies courage directed in service of the common good.

Courage forms the heart of the common good leadership model and fuels the other six practices. The word *courage* derives from the French *coeur*, meaning heart. Heart in this case does not refer to the organ that pumps blood but to the vital center in each of us from which our choices and actions reverberate out into the world. Without courage, we might have a good model for leadership but may not be able to put it into action. Moreover, as a leader engages in the other six practices they become resources that feed her courage. Thus the model is like a circulatory system—courage feeds and is fed by the other practices.

Courage differs from fearlessness. As Ambrose Redmoon, author and activist, says, "Courage is not the absence of fear, but rather the judgment that something else is more important than fear."[3] Fear is an instinctual response to threatening stimuli involving the most ancient part of our brain, the brainstem or "reptilian" brain, and triggering the fight-or-flight response. Humans have the capacity to override the reptilian brain's fear response and listen to the more reasoned response that comes from the neocortex, the part of the brain capable of abstraction, planning, and conscious thought. Courage is largely a matter of responding to life circumstances with choices that flow from that place of higher-order reasoning.

Thus a person can be filled with fear and still choose courage. Courage is the capacity to move forward even when the bells and buzzers of our self- and social-oriented survival instincts are telling us to sit down and be quiet. In fact, courageous people know fear more intimately than most because they face their fears and overcome them on a regular basis, while others who are unconscious of their fears remain incapable of acting. Courage begins with recognizing our fears and continues with our stepping right into them, saying, "I am afraid *and* I will move ahead anyway because I know what is right." Martin Luther King Jr.'s colleagues report that even though he was preoccupied with the fear of death almost every day, he still took action for civil rights.

FORMS OF COURAGE

The form of courage that is most often required of leadership for the common good is moral courage. Moral courage is willingness to do the right thing when the wrong thing is easier and less costly. When leaders are facing resistance and find themselves caught between their commitment to the change agenda and their instinct for self-preservation and first- and second-circle concerns, what supports them in maintaining a third-circle orientation is moral courage.

Because they can be personally costly, however, actions based on moral courage are rare events. Robert Kennedy commented: "Few people are willing to brave the disapproval of their fellows, the censure of their colleagues, the wrath of their society. Moral courage is a rarer commodity than bravery in battle or great intelligence. Yet it is the one essential vital quality of those who seek to change a world, which yields most painfully to change."[4]

Moral courage is like a stem cell form of courage. From moral courage are generated other expressions of courage as required in all dimensions of a leader's life—such as social, emotional, intellectual, physical, political, and spiritual courage. Leaders express social courage by standing up for what they believe among their peers, at family get-togethers, at neighborhood gatherings, and in meetings with professional colleagues. In doing so they liberate themselves from undue peer pressure and live undistracted third-circle lives.

Leaders show emotional courage when they allow their feelings about injustice to infuse their communications. For example, Ray Williams, a Native American leader who lives in the state of Washington, represents native concerns in meetings across the United States and around the world. When he speaks of the challenges of his people, he often weeps, transforming the hearts of his listeners and thereby reweaving the connections between native and non-native peoples.

Leaders practice intellectual courage every time they ask difficult questions for the sake of the common good, such as: What can we do to promote greater gender equity in this institution? How will we manage our local water resources for the sake of salmon and people? What would a just global economic community look like? Or how can we provide a basic education to every child on the planet?

Leaders practice physical courage when they endure physical hardships because of their work for the common good. For example, Suu Kyi showed physical courage during Burmese protests in the midst of armed soldiers and also during the many years she was under house arrest. So did the protestors in Egypt, Tunis, and

Libya in 2011, who knew they would pay a physical price for publicly advocating for democratic reform. On a local level, it takes physical courage to start a neighborhood watch program to reduce crime by getting rid of crack houses.

Leaders practice political courage when they are willing to spend political capital on issues that matter and deal with the consequences. The leaders who spoke up for abolition in 1850, opposed the Vietnam War in 1964, and resisted going to war with Iraq in 2003 all practiced political courage.

Leaders practice spiritual courage by caring deeply enough about their faith and spiritual traditions to declare and commit to them openly. Further, spiritual courage is required to recognize that Spirit is the author of many faith stories and that we must therefore put aside religious differences when working for the common good and acknowledge how moral purpose binds the many faith stories together.

As it turns out, moral courage can cost a person plenty—in Suu Kyi's case, years of imprisonment and house arrest. In other cases, it can lead to torture during imprisonment, as it did for U.S. civil rights activist Fannie Lou Hamer, or even death, as with Benazir Bhutto and Mahatma Gandhi. Most of us will not face risks of this scale, yet even in the most ordinary life circumstances people often pay a price for moral courage. For example, speaking up about a controversial issue in the neighborhood may elicit ridicule from the neighbors. Or being the one to raise the difficult question at the office could cost someone their job or limit their career.

Because courageous leadership can be costly, it is important to know how to renew our courage. One essential source of courage is personal core values. Suu Kyi underscores this connection in her speech "Freedom from Fear," written in 1990: "The wellspring of courage and endurance in the face of unbridled power is generally a firm belief in the sanctity of ethical principles. . . . It is man's vision of a world fit for rational, civilized humanity, which leads him to dare and to suffer to build societies free from want and fear. Concepts such as truth, justice, and compassion cannot be dismissed as trite when these are often the only bulwarks which stand against ruthless power."[5]

People with moral courage are often compelled to ask, "What do my core values ask of me in this situation?" and the important follow-up question, "Knowing that my actions might be costly, why do it anyway?" In response, some reply:

"Because it is the right thing to do."
"For my children and grandchildren."
"Because I want to be able to look myself in the eye in the mirror."
"Now that I know, how could I spend my life on anything less?
"If not me, then who?"

When leaders are aware of the call of their core values in a given situation and reflect on why they will follow the call despite possible negative consequences, they exhibit moral courage.

COURAGE AS A VIRTUE

The fact that courage has long been considered one of the classical virtues offers insights into its nature. Aristotle regarded courage as first among all virtues because it takes courage to put the other virtues into action.[6] In addition, Thomas Aquinas, building on the work of Aristotle, placed courage alongside justice, prudence, and temperance, as one of the four cardinal virtues fundamental to all virtuous behavior.[7]

The word *cardinal* is from the Latin word *cardes*, meaning hinge. A cardinal virtue allows access to the development of all other virtues.

Virtues are expressions of moral excellence developed through practice. Virtues are made up of habits, and habits are constructed from individual moral choices. A virtue is composed of countless single moral choices that when woven together become substantial enough to bear a lot of weight. To better understand this idea, imagine moral principles as strands of fiber. As a person makes moral choices and lives them on a daily basis, those individual choices twine together to form a rope—a habit. As habits are practiced over time, the ropes twine together to become a cable—a virtue.

When asked how one develops courage, Aristotle in essence responded: How does one become a good cobbler? By making shoes. How does one become a good shipwright? By building ships. How does one become courageous? By acting courageously.[8] Leaders develop the virtues they practice every day. Conversely, leaders become depraved by behaving immorally every day, affecting the moral fabric of their society.

A virtue, according to Aristotle, is a middle path. In this context, courage is a middle way between recklessness and cowardice—between taking action foolishly and taking no action when action is needed. Thus courage is a reasoned approach to taking action, involving strategy, astuteness, and prudent use of resources.

For example, a member of a CEO's executive team might decide to challenge a questionable institutional practice—such as giving indulgent executive team bonuses—using courage as a middle way between recklessness and cowardice. Knowing the policy was instituted by the CEO himself, she might decide to talk to the boss privately rather than impetuously raising the concern during a team meeting. She might also choose to use wisdom and humility in her approach, rather than thoughtlessly critiquing her boss. In the meeting with the CEO, she might present her concern in the form of two requests: "Can you tell me the history behind our executive compensation policy?" and "I have been noticing some unintended consequences of the original policy and would like to explore them with you." Not wanting to let cowardice manifest in the form of procrastination, she could add, "When is a good time to get together and explore this question?" Rather than sitting on a difficult issue or rushing in where angels fear to tread, she finds a middle way strategically tailored for the occasion.

An example of the strategic use of the middle way of courage applied on a larger scale is the Salt March led by Mahatma Gandhi in 1930. This three-week protest march from Gandhi's ashram to the seashore to collect salt was a public protest of the salt tax imposed by the colonial government and the beginning of the larger protest of British rule. Gandhi made some strategic choices concerning the march. He realized it would provoke the colonial government to respond with force, which would bring international attention to India's movement for independence. He also knew it was a compassionate choice because everyone in India used salt and because the tax was hurting the poor the most. In addition, he designed the march to make participation in it possible for the vast numbers of people, since India has plenty of oceanfront and anyone could make salt.

While the middle way is usually best, the urgency of today's social, economic, and environmental challenges calls us to be bolder in our actions. For too long, humanity's collective courage on behalf of the common good has generally leaned toward timidity. But considering the "fierce urgency of now" the needle should be tipped slightly, with great care, in the direction of recklessness to extend freedom to all, end hunger, relieve thirst, end war, reverse global warming, and leave a legacy worthy of our grandchildren's dreams and aspirations.

COURAGE AND THE OTHER SIX COMMON GOOD LEADERSHIP PRACTICES

Courage, situated at the center of the common good leadership practices model, reverberates through the model like a heartbeat, providing energy to each of the other six practices. It takes courage to align our lives with our core values; to open ourselves to experience the margins; to sit in the tension between what is and what ought to be until a vision is born; to dedicate ourselves to inclusiveness in the form of gracious space; to claim our voice and then speak the truth in love to power; and to walk into the most difficult questions on our watch, whether or not we have received the gift of hope. None of these six practices is casual advice. Each one is an invitation to consciously choose the challenges associated with purposeful and intentional living.

Moreover, the model is cyclic. In developing skills supporting leadership for the common good, leaders move around the circle of practices not once but many times. Courage assists them in beginning every cycle as an opportunity to deepen each practice. It is as if courage asks: This time when you commit to values, will you follow them into the conversations and the places where you would rather not go? This time when you go to margins, will you stay longer and listen more deeply? This time while cocreating gracious space, will you stretch a little further as you invite strangers? This time when you proclaim your vision, will you engage power with truth and love in a more compelling way? This time will you venture further into the core of the issue, in pursuit of change for the common good?

Each time we circumnavigate the model by doing the practices, we have a chance to mature as leaders for the common good. In this way, leadership grows through practice, a phenomenon that holds true for all leaders, even those we regard as icons of leadership.

For example, Martin Luther King Jr. had embraced nonviolence as a methodology from the beginning of his career, but only over time did he grow into living it deeply. Because his life was constantly threatened, local civil rights activists in Montgomery encouraged him to keep guns in various places around his house. On Sunday night, February 26, 1956, Bayard Rustin, the black civil right activist from New York who counseled King on principles of nonviolence, visited him and his wife, Coretta, in the parlor of their home.

When Rustin learned about the guns throughout the house, he challenged his host. Rustin asserted that even though King was planting seeds of nonviolence in the movement, the presence of guns was a violation of those teachings and would limit his and the movement's effectiveness. Author Stewart Burns captures the exchange that followed between Rustin and King:

> "The Movement is non-violent," King replied stiffly. "We're not going to harm anybody unless they harm us." . . . But he believed that black people had the right to defend their homes and families. Ruston responded that in this historic situation such rights were trumped by a greater moral responsibility. A commitment to Gandhian nonviolence called for unconditional rejection of retaliation, even in self-defense. . . .
>
> Rustin asserted, two decades after King's death, . . . "The glorious thing is that he (King) came to a profoundly deep understanding of non-violence through the struggle itself," and through reading and discussions which he had in the process of carrying out the protests.[9]

Courage and the six other practices reinforce one another. Each one of these six practices, when engaged, fosters the development of courage in the leader. As courage flows into the six other practices and we work with them repeatedly, we build up a reservoir of experience with them. Then those reservoirs of experience are available to us as assets to draw from when courage is needed. Engaging the practices is very much like going to the gym daily to build muscle so courage is available when needed.

Aligning with our personal core values roots us in the third circle, where courageous choices, while not easier, are more obvious. When the right choice is obvious, it fills us with internal conviction that we must act. Further, because our core values are a deep expression of our authentic selves, we become inspired to courageously embody those values for the sake of our integrity.

Embracing the wisdom of the margins builds a sense of solidarity with those who are enduring injustice and hardship. Solidarity inspires courageous action because when suffering has a name and a face, leaders are emboldened to act out of empathy.

Crafting a vision—a picture of what could be—stirs our hearts and moves us to courageous action. It is also true that with a vision our moral conviction flourishes, leading to courageous action.

Creating gracious space, an environment marked by inclusiveness and openness, allows all members of a group, including the leader, to courageously raise difficult questions, knowing the group has the best interest of all its members at heart. Gracious space provides an ideal environment for people to practice courage, and in the process they develop courageous habits that can be practiced anywhere.

Claiming voice and thus answering a call can provide leaders with the courage necessary to act on a vision. For example, when Suu Kyi claimed her voice as leader of the democracy movement of Burma and received 82 percent of the popular vote in 1990, her courage was informed not just by a personal response to injustice but also by the call of national leadership.

When leaders receive hope in their dark moments, it refuels their hearts with courage to keep going. In Spirit's company, leaders' hearts are quickened by hope, and new storehouses of courage are discovered and employed.

Spirit plays a vital role in the development of courage, as can be seen in the lives of many transformational leaders, especially those associated with the religious sector, such as Mother Teresa, Thich Nhat Hanh, and Archbishop Desmond Tutu. But Spirit has also been an important source of courage for individuals in many other sectors. Former president of Poland and trade union leader Lech Walesa attributes his courage to his Catholic faith. And a spiritual vision gave Sojourner Truth the "perfect trust in God and prayer" that fueled her remarkable career as a black American abolitionist and women's rights activist in the mid-nineteenth century.[10] Spirit becomes a source of courage through daily personal spiritual practice. When a relationship with Spirit is nurtured by leaders, they become increasingly influenced by the divine call to work for the common good.

PRACTICING COURAGE

While leaders can practice courage in the context of the other six practices, courage can and should also be practiced in its own right. If we want better upper body strength, we know where to go and what to do. But where is the courage gym? What can leaders do to practice courage? Eleanor Roosevelt answered this when she said, "We gain strength, and courage, and confidence by each experience in which we really stop to look fear in the face. . . . We must do that which we think we cannot."[11]

Each time we face our fears and take a step forward to initiate change despite those fears, we build our courage. The first time we act with courage, it may be difficult. The second time may seem even harder, because we remember how awkward it felt the first time. But the one-hundredth time we act with courage, it will be much easier, as illustrated by the following story. A woman organized, led, and then spoke at a human rights rally. After her speech, another woman came up to congratulate her and said, "I would give anything to be able to speak out about my beliefs publicly like you just did." The woman replied, "Would you be willing to speak at 1,253 rallies?"

Similarly, Jeffrey Wigand, a former researcher at Brown and Williamson Tobacco Company whose story was made famous in the movie *The Insider,* exemplifies a leader who developed courage to a high degree. Drawing on his moral courage, he became a whistle-blower for an entire industry, exposing the intentional harm and deceit perpetrated on the public by the tobacco companies, in spite of losing his job and facing lawsuits and death threats.

The best way to begin building courage is to practice courage in small ways in daily life, preparing ourselves to face bigger challenges when they come. What takes courage for you to do may not require courage for another person since everyone's background and psychology are different. The important thing is to consistently foster courage by practicing behavior that evokes fear within you but you know must be done. Each time we act with courage in any setting, we increase in confidence to act with courage in all settings.

To build courage, we can also refer to our experiences with courage, which includes the experiences of others we have observed or read about. History is filled with stories of exceptional people whose courage can inspire us, such as the behavior of Dietrich Bonhoeffer, Mary McLeod Bethune, Oscar Romero, César Chávez, and Chief Joseph. Sources of courage can be fictional as well. Sam in J.R.R. Tolkien's *Lord of the Rings* displays extreme moral courage as he helps Frodo avoid the temptations of the Ring. Sydney Carton in Charles Dickens's *Tale of Two Cities* also exemplifies moral courage taken to a sacrificial level when he offers his life for a friend, saying, "It is a far, far better thing that I do, than I have ever done."[12]

In her speech entitled "Freedom from Fear," Suu Kyi aptly states that courage comes from developing the habit of not letting fear dictate one's actions: "Fearlessness may be a gift but perhaps more precious is the courage acquired through endeavor, courage that comes from cultivating the habit of refusing to let fear dictate one's actions, courage that could be described as 'grace under pressure'—grace which is renewed repeatedly in the face of harsh, unremitting pressure."[13] As courage grows, it reverberates through our choices and actions, increasing our capacity to be leaders for the common good.

EXERCISES
Practicing Courage

Identify a challenging situation you are facing that according to your core values requires action but which might be costly.

Next, reflect on the question Why do it anyway? List at least three reasons.

Finally, listen to your heart to see if one of these responses has the power to deepen your courage to act in alignment with your core values. To affirm this new reason to be courageous, speak it out loud to a friend or write it down.

REFLECTION QUESTIONS

* In your life, what is more important than fear?

* What are three ways you could practice acting with courage in your day-to-day life?

* As you think about the common good leadership model, which of the seven practices of common good leadership causes you the most anxiety?

* What three steps can you take to gain the courage to practice it?

JUSTICE IS WHAT
LOVE LOOKS LIKE
IN PUBLIC.
–Cornel West

Looking Forward
A Movement for the Common Good

SHARING THE ROCK is a way of living that honors all life and promotes equity, love, and peace among people. Making it the primary framework for our daily choice-making is the central work of our time. The practice of leadership for the common good is essential for sharing the rock, for bringing us to that day when all will enjoy the fruits of a caring and just society. It is not complicated work; we need only remain conscious of staying in the third circle. Each day every person, institution, and community can decide which of the three circles will govern their behavior. Because the third circle is the sole territory of the common good, it remains the only circle on which leaders for the common good need to focus.

Although leadership for the common good is uncomplicated, it is difficult, requiring us to summon internal and external allies. Internally, we are supported by our core values, our compassion born of experience on the margins, and our vision of what ought to be, all of which root us in principled choice-making. Externally, we reach out to allies in gracious space, trusting that the path to the common good is filled with diverse individuals who will find a way to work together despite their differences.

Having gathered our allies, we claim our voice. We move into the difficult issues of our time trusting that we will receive hope and confident that our courage will grow as we continue on.

Throughout, we remember the power of community in creating social change and associate with like-minded individuals for support in our daily practice of leadership for the common good. Social change happens most rapidly when like-minded individuals act together. According to sociologists, it takes only 5 percent of any group moving together in a new direction to be considered a movement. Thus a surprisingly small number of us may be enough to catalyze a social innovation or movement, perhaps in our neighborhoods, at our workplaces, or on our Facebook pages.

ESSENTIAL ASPECTS OF SOCIAL MOVEMENT LEADERSHIP

The essential aspects of social movement leadership dovetail well with the practices of leadership for the common good. A social movement is the weaving together of simultaneous acts of innovation and reform in many settings into a coordinated expression of power and intention focused on a common social concern. Local innovations and reforms, if shared and replicated, can spread the movement to other areas and thus help it grow exponentially. Movements begin by a leader articulating a principle-based unifying vision and inviting the cocreation of gracious space, where all feel welcome to participate in the movement in ways that honor their interests. The leader then fosters hope and courage among participants to maintain the movement's momentum and, through his behavior, encourages others.

Social movement leaders must also promote inclusiveness and decentralize power so that anyone anywhere in the movement has the power to invite others to join. Social movements honor the third-circle orientation by encouraging all to participate, placing power in the hands of everyone involved, and focusing on the common good. Social movements are built on the passions and talents of many and are not dependent on charismatic saviors. Charismatic leaders can be assassinated, but movements cannot. Today, social movement leaders can use the modern tool of social networking to ensure diverse input, speed up the movement-building process, and increase a movement's power to effect change for the common good. Social movement leaders must also encourage all members of the movement to find their voice relative to the vision so that progress toward putting the vision into action increases daily while all members remain focused on a common goal.

The most successful social movement leaders build infrastructures that allow for an ongoing dialogue between local and regional or national leaders. In this way, successful grassroots initiatives can inform regional or national public policy reforms related to the movement while creating a pipeline for such reforms to take root in local communities.

Like leaders for the common good, social movement leaders must also anticipate resistance and inspire movement members to continue to claim their voice in love despite any opposition. All of these essential aspects of social movement leadership require sharing of information and power, as well as trusting that people can work together in gracious space for the good of all.

THE URGENCY OF ACTING NOW

In these times of dire challenges and momentous opportunities, we are charged with a moral obligation to do what we can where we can—a mission we commit to by deciding what we are willing to do today for the next generation and for people living on earth five hundred years from now.

It's time to take three practical steps on behalf of the common good. It's also time to find "accountability buddies" who will care enough about us and the future to ask us at the end of each month: "What did you do this month to honor your values, claim your voice, and act with courage?" We never know whether our next action might be the one that unleashes the waters of reform, sending that flow out of our little corner of the world to cascade into a global movement for the common good.

In addition, it's time to set up camp in the third circle—the place of principle and inclusiveness, home to the common good—and share our campfire with the very next person who comes along. As we move forward in good company, supporting one another and picking each other up after falling, it is important to celebrate those occasions when our conscious choices as leaders on behalf of the common good catalyze a change, big or small.

The following list of practical actions taken in our communities, regions, and our nation could further propel changes for the common good:

* The United Nations could issue an urgent plea to all national leaders to honor the Universal Declaration of Human Rights and to draft a plan for how their nation intends to advance the common good at home and abroad in the next decade.

* The president of the United States could draft a Compact for the Common Good and ask all citizens, leaders, institutions, and civic groups to become active stewards of the common good.

* Congress could issue a challenge to its members to publicly examine how each bill they consider adds or detracts from the common good.

* Governors could use their voices to demand action so that every corner of their state becomes a safe place for the human community and the environment to flourish.

* Every mayor and city council could make a clarion call to the city's citizens and institutions to find practical ways to serve as

stewards of the common good in their families, neighborhoods, schools, and local institutions.

* Every church, synagogue, and mosque could write a Confessing Statement urging local, state, and federal government, corporations, and all seats of power to respond now to the injustices on their watch and, through the power of care, justice, and inclusion, advocate for a future characterized by the good of all.

* Every scout troop could ask all scouts and their parents to take collective civic action to remedy local injustices.

* Every school, college, and university, public and private, could host a day of learning, to discuss what it means to be active stewards of the common good and encourage students and faculty to take practical action.

* Every library could create a display that encourages patrons to inquire about the common good in their corner of the world and take effective action to realize it.

* Every professional organization, from accountants to zoologists, could raise the issue of the common good among their peers and inspire them to serve as stewards of the common good.

* Every chamber of commerce, business round-table, and other organization that supports commerce could inspire entrepreneurs to think about how market forces can be used to advance the common good.

* Service clubs throughout the nation, such as Rotary, Kiwanis, and Lions clubs, could examine how they can become more powerful advocates for justice in their communities.

* Every Red Cross volunteer, member of the armed forces, op-ed page editor, nanny, and blogger could assess how they might advance the common good in their activities.

Such work is challenging, but it also keeps us feeling good because it connects us to good work, good people, and Spirit's own goodness. This is surely what humans are created for, since nothing makes us happier than living a courageous public life as a steward of the common good.

Acknowledgments

ALTHOUGH THIS BOOK REPRESENTS a view of leadership that has been incubating in me for a long time, publishing it required integrating ideas and finding professionals who could edit the manuscript and arrange for various aspects of production. In general, I am indebted to many students, seminar participants, and colleagues who have placed their thumbprint on these teachings over the years. I am grateful as well to a number of people who helped in the book's preparation and production. Larry Pennings's clear thinking and provocative questions helped shape the content of this book. Craig Comstock provided advice on the structure of the book and edited "The Rock" story.

Carolyn Bond served as a tireless main editor of the book and helped me weave years of experience into an integrated manuscript while holding me and the text in gracious space. Her authentic curiosity and powerful intuition helped her shape vital questions that challenged me to relentlessly pursue and clarify my deepest beliefs. This book would also not have come to fruition without the fun-loving spirit and wise counsel of Ellen Kleiner of Blessingway Authors' Services, who provided a highly skilled copyedit and coached me on advantageous choices to give this self-published book a professional touch and make it widely available to readers. In addition, Ann Lowe did incredible work on the cover and interior designs, capturing the spirit of the book.

Finally, I wish to acknowledge two sources of love and support that have contributed to this book. First, I offer thanks to Spirit, who has given me the tongue of a teacher to sustain the weary with a word and who meets me morning after morning with love, hope, and inspiration. Second, the love I feel from Spirit has been manifest over the past thirty-two years in the laughter, forgiveness, and incredible kindness I have received without merit from my wife, Sandy, who naturally possesses the kind of practical wisdom it has taken me almost a lifetime to understand and express in this book.

Notes

Chapter 1. Shifting to a Common Good Worldview

1. http://en.wikipedia.org/wiki/Earthrise.

2. Robert Sullivan, *100 Photographs that Changed the World* (New York: Life, 2003), http://en.wikipedia.org/wiki/Earthrise.

3. Martin Luther King Jr., "Letter from a Birmingham Jail" (April 16, 1963), http://mlkkpp01.stanford.edu/index.php/resources/article/annotated_letter_from_birmingham/.

4. Stewart Brand, "Photography Changes Our Relationship to Our Planet," http://click.si.edu/Story.aspx?story=31.

5. Joanna Macy, "Reflections on Our Moment in History, *Earth Light: A Magazine of Spiritual Ecology*, http://www.earthlight.org/jmacyessay.html.

6. Millennium Development Goals, http://www.un.org/millenniumgoals/.

7. Balle's Vision, http://www.livingeconomies.org/aboutus/mission-and-principles.

8. Fairtrade Labelling Organizations International, *FLO International: Annual Report 2007* (URL accessed on June 16, 2008), http://en.wikipedia.org/wiki/Fair_trade.

Chapter 2. Living from the Third Circle

1. Lawrence Kohlberg, *The Philosophy of Moral Development: Moral Stages and the Idea of Justice*, vol. 1 (New York: Harper & Row), 1981.

2. Carol Gilligan, *In a Different Voice* (Cambridge: Harvard University Press), 1982.

3. The three-circle diagram is adapted from the work of Tim McMahon of the Holden Leadership Center, University of Oregon. McMahon, in his representation of the work of Kohlberg and Gilligan, labels the three circles "Self," "Others," and "Principle."

4. Thomas Thatcher Graves (1841–1893) was aide to General Godfrey Weitzel, who took command of the city of Richmond, Virginia, on April 2, 1865. Graves wrote many years later that Lincoln said to Weitzel on April 4, regarding how to treat the people of Richmond, "If I were in your place, I'd let 'em up easy, let 'em up easy." Graves's manuscript containing this quote is in the John Nicolay Papers at the Abraham Lincoln Presidential Library and Museum, Springfield, Illinois. For this source I thank James Cornelius, curator of the Lincoln Collection at the Abraham Lincoln Presidential Library and Museum. Correspondence received March 2, 2011.

5. Abraham Lincoln, Gettysburg Address (November 20, 1863), http://www.usconstitution.net/getty.html.

6. Alexis de Tocqueville, *Democracy in America*, vol. II (Ware, Hertfordshire, England: Wordsworth Editions, 1998), 230.

7. http://www.worldlingo.com/ma/enwiki/en/Potlatch.

8. Leymah Roberta Gbowee, Liberian peace activist, is credited with offering this translation of *ubuntu*, http://en.wikiquote.org/wiki/Leymah_Gbowee.

9. http://en.wikipedia.org/wiki/Ubuntu_(philosophy).

10. Ron Heifetz, *Leadership without Easy Answers* (Cambridge: Harvard University Press, 1998).

Chapter 3. Reframing Leadership

1. Martin Luther King Jr., "Letter from a Birmingham Jail" (April 16, 1963), http://mlkkpp01.stanford.edu/index.php/resources/article/annotated_letter_from_birmingham/.

2. http://www.now.org/issues/title_ix/index.html.

3. http://www.titlenine.com/category/who+are+we/title+ix-+what+is+it-.do.

4. Doctors Without Borders, http://www.doctorswithout border.org/aboutus/.

5. Edwin Markham, "Outwitted," in *The Shoes of Happiness and Other Poems: The Third Book of Verse* (Garden City, NY: Doubleday, Page & Co., 1919), 1.

6. Martin Luther King Jr., "Beyond Vietnam: A Time to Break Silence" (speech, Riverside Church, New York, April 4, 1967), http://www.americanrhetoric.com/speeches/mlkatimetobreaksilence.htm.

7. Frances Moore Lappé, "The City that Ended Hunger," http://www.yesmagazine.org/issues/food-for-everyone/the-city-that-ended-hunger.

8. http://www.solarviews.com/eng/apo13.htm#survival.

Chapter 4. Choosing Your Personal Values

1. Nelson Mandela (Rivonia Trial speech, April 20, 1964), http://db.nelsonmandela.org/speeches/pub_view.asp?pg=item&ItemID=NMS010&txtstr=rivonia.

2. Ibid.

3. Nelson Mandela (inaugural address, May 10, 1994), http://db.nelsonmandela.org/speeches/pub_view.asp?pg=item&ItemID=NMS176&txtstr=inauguration. Biography based in part on http://www.nelsonmandela.org/index.php/memory/views/biography/.

4. Aaron Feuerstein, interviewed in "The Mensch of Malden Mills," an episode of the CBS news program *60 Minutes* (July 6,

2003), http://www.cbsnews.com/stories/2003/07/03/60minutes/main561656.shtml.

5. *Parade Magazine* (1996), http://en.wikipedia.org/wiki/Aaron_Feuerstein.

6. See Note 4.

7. See Note 1.

8. Ibid.

9. "Mandela Admits ANC Violated Rights, Too," *Financial Times* (November 2, 1998), http://en.wikipedia.org/wiki/Nelson_Mandela.

10. Author unknown, http://www.sapphyr.net/natam/two-wolves.htm.

Chapter 5. Embracing the Wisdom of the Margins

1. Sarah Bradford, *Harriet Tubman: The Moses of Her People* (New York: Kenniston, 1962). Details of Harriet Tubman's story vary from source to source.

2. Martin Luther King Jr., "Beyond Vietnam: A Time to Break Silence" (speech, Riverside Church, New York, April 4, 1967), http://www.americanrhetoric.com/speeches/mlkatimetobreaksilence.htm.

3. This idea and the following discussion are based on William Perry's observation that people respond to challenge by retreating to an earlier time, escaping, or staying and struggling.

4. Hans Magnus Enzenberger, "song for those who know," in *Selected Poems* (Riverdale, NY: Sheep Meadow Press, 1999), 95.

5. James Hollis, *Finding Meaning in the Second Half of Life: How to Finally Really Grow Up* (New York: Penguin, 2005).

6. Robert Terry, *For Whites Only* (Grand Rapids, MI: William B. Eerdsman, 1975).

Chapter 6. Crafting a Vision

1. Muhammad Yunus, *Banker to the Poor: Micro-Lending and the Battle against World Poverty* (New York: PublicAffairs, 1999), ix.

2. http://nobelprize.org/nobel_prizes/peace/laureates/2006/press.html.

3. George Bernard Shaw's original citation reads: "You see things; and you say, 'Why?' But I dream things that never were; and I say, 'Why not?'" *Back to Methuselah,* act I, *Selected Plays with Prefaces,* vol. 2 (New York: Dodd, Mead, 1949), 7.

4. http://www.myhero.com/go/hero.asp?hero= RYAN HREL-JAC.

5. Tekio Sogen Rotaishi, founder of Chozen-ji Zen Dojo, Honolulu, Hawaii, at a retreat on the Buddhist view of leadership, sponsored by the Kellogg Foundation (Honolulu, Hawaii, 2001). The author was present.

6. Daniel H. Burnham, "Make No Little Plans" (speech, Town Planning Conference, London, October 1910).

7. http://www.kiva.org/about/history.

Chapter 7. Creating Gracious Space

1. http://en.wikipedia.org/wiki/Fred_Rogers.

2. Both the video and the transcript of Fred Rogers' testimony are available at http://www.americanrhetoric.com/speeches/fredrogerssenatetcstimonypbs.htm.

3. Adapted from a handout by the Center for Ethical Leadership, Seattle, Washington.

Chapter 8. Claiming Your Voice

1. http://www.orrt.org/oliver/.

2. Mary Oliver, "The Journey," in *Dream Work* (New York: Grove Atlantic, 1986), 38–39.

3. http://www.goodreads.com/author/quotes/56230. Howard_Thurman.

4. *Life Positive* (March 2002), http://www.lifepositive.com/body/nature/environmental.asp.

5. W. H. Murray, *The Scottish Himalayan Expedition* (London: Dent, 1951), http://en.wikipedia.org/wiki/W._H._Murray. According to the article, the passage occurs "near the beginning" of the book.

6. http://www.greatsite.com/timeline-english-bible-history/martin-luther.html.

7. Thomas Hardy, "In Tenebris—II," in *Thomas Hardy: The Complete Poems* (New York: Palgrave, 2001), 168.

8. Michael Edwards, "Networks for Social Change" (speech, New York, October 17, 2008), http://www.opendemocracy.net/globalization-vision_reflections/love_3149.jsp?time=1232332687.

9. http://www.washingtonpost.com/wp-srv/politics/daily/sept98/wallace031795.htm.

10. Ibid.

Chapter 9. Receiving Hope

1. Stewart Burns, *To the Mountaintop* (San Francisco: HarperSanFrancisco, 2004), 39.

2. Joan Chittister, *Scarred by Struggle, Transformed by Hope* (Grand Rapids, MI: William B. Eerdmans), 107.

3. Vaclav Havel, *Disturbing the Peace* (New York: Vintage Books, 1990), 181.

4. Emily Dickinson, "Hope Is the Thing with Feathers," in *The Poems of Emily Dickinson*, Thomas H. Johnson, ed. (Cambridge, MA: The Belknap Press of Harvard University Press, 1983), 140.

5. See Note 3.

6. "The Shadow of the Past," *Fellowship of the Ring,* DVD, directed by Peter Jackson (Burbank, CA: New Line Home Entertainment, 2001).

7. http://www.crossroad.to/Persecution/Bonhoffer.html.

8. See Note 1, 82.

9. Elie Wiesel, *Night* (New York: Avon Books, 1982), 106–7.

10. Abraham Lincoln, "Gettysburg Address" (speech, November 20, 1863), http://www.usconstitution.net/getty.html.

11. Winston Churchill, "This Was Their Finest Hour" (speech, June 18, 1940), http://www.historyplace.com/speeches/churchill-hour.htm.

12. The lyrics, written as a poem by James Weldon Johnson in 1899, were first recited on Abraham Lincoln's birthday in 1900. The poet's brother, John Rosamond H. Johnson, set the poem to music in 1905, http://en.wikipedia.org/wiki/Lift_Every_Voice_and_Sing.

13. Norman Cousins, http://thinkexist.com/quotation/the_capacity_for_hope_is_the_most_significant/151350.html.

14. http://quotationsbook.com/quote/46207/#axzz1KSspT47Y.

15. Martin Luther King Jr., Nobel Prize Acceptance Speech (Oslo, Norway, December 10, 1964), http://nobelprize.org/nobel_prizes/peace/laureates/1964/king-acceptance.html.

Chapter 10. Acting with Courage

1. Irwin Abrams, *The Nobel Prize Annual, 1991* (New York: IMG, 1992), 77–85, http://www.irwinabrams.com/books/excerpts/annual91.html.

2. Aung San Suu Kyi, "Freedom from Fear" (acceptance speech, Sakharov Prize for Freedom of Thought, July 1991), http://www.thirdworldtraveler.com/Burma/FreedomFromFearSpeech.html.

3. Ambrose Redmoon, "No Peaceful Warriors," *Gnosis: A Journal of the Western Inner Traditions* 21 (Fall 1991): 40.

4. Robert F. Kennedy, Day of Affirmation Address (June 6, 1966), http://www.jfklibrary.org/Historical+Resources/Archives/Reference+Desk/Speeches/RFK/Day+of+Affirmation+Address+News+Release.htm.

5. See Note 2.

6. Aristotle, *Nicomachean Ethics*, book II (New York: Oxford University Press, 1998).

7. Thomas Aquinas, *Summa Theologica* (New York Benziger Brothers, 1948), 846.

8. See Note 6, ch. 1.

9. Stewart Burns, *To the Mountaintop* (San Francisco, Harper SanFrancisco, 2004), 82.

10. Sojourner Truth, "Who Was Sojourner Truth?" http://www.sojournertruthmemorial.org/history.html.

11. Eleanor Roosevelt, *You Learn by Living* (New York: Harper, 1960), 29.

12. Charles Dickens, *A Tale of Two Cities* (New York: Penguin, 1960), 367.

13. See Note 2.

About the Author

BILL GRACE is a social justice activist, traveling teacher, and architect of ideas. From 1976 to 1991, he served in higher education, promoting ideas related to moral and civic responsibility, service learning, and global citizenship.

In 1991, he founded the Seattle-based Center for Ethical Leadership, a nonprofit organization dedicated to promoting the common good through ethical leadership, civic responsibility, and collaborative problem-solving. During his fourteen-year tenure as executive director, the center developed a national reputation for its innovative, inspired leadership development programs.

Bill's current research and writing focus on the development of Spirit-inspired leadership to call forth the wisdom, courage, and hope needed in these times. Believing that leadership must be grounded in a global sense of the common good, he promotes leadership and social action that focuses on spiritual development, inclusiveness, and moral courage in pursuit of a just and peaceful world.

Director of Common Good Works (www.commongoodworks. com), Bill speaks and leads seminars around the world.

Order Form

Quantity   Amount

_____ *Sharing the Rock: Shaping Our Future through Leadership*   _____
              for the Common Good ($17.00)

                          Sales tax of 0.95% for Washington State residents _____

                                  Shipping and handling ($3.00 for first book; _____

                                          $1.00 for each additional book) _____

                                                Total amount enclosed _____

Quantity discounts available

Method of payment:

Check or money order enclosed (made payable to Common Good Works
in US funds only)

❏ MasterCard   ❏ VISA

Credit Card #:_____Exp.:_____

Ship to (please print):

Name_____

Address _____

City/State/Zip _____

Phone_____

commongood

Common Good Works
14216 SE Eastgate Drive
Bellevue, WA 98006
www.commongoodworks.com